Healing & Happiness After Stroke

How to Get Back Up After Life
Turned Upside-Down

Kari Dahlgren

First Edition: November 2016

ISBN: 978-0-9983716-0-3

Edited by: Daniel K. Zondervan, Ph.D

Cover by: Phoenix by iStock.com/Apola, Calligraphy by Jenny Famularcano and Kari Dahlgren, Cover Design by Kari Dahlgren

www.FlintRehab.com

Special thanks to stroke survivors
Pamela Hsieh and Terry Stevens

Table of Contents

A Mini Love Story

To make a successful recovery after stroke, you have to fall in love with the process.

At first, it can feel impossible to love after your life has been turned upside-down, but it's a must. Stroke recovery needs love in order to move.

Similar to any good relationship, loving your recovery requires patience, understanding, and respect. It's a two-way street.

If you become committed to your recovery, then your recovery will become committed to you. If you put the time and effort into nurturing your recovery, your recovery will return the favor.

If you love your recovery, your recovery will love you back.

But you can only get there by loving yourself *first*.

This book will guide you through the steps that love requires. You'll learn how to manage life's new variables and develop a deep understanding of yourself.

Then you'll know exactly what it takes to find healing and happiness after stroke.

Chapter 1
Leaning into Love

"Love yourself first and everything else falls into line. You really have to love yourself to get anything done in this world."

–Lucille Ball

To recover from stroke, you need to heal both the head *and the heart*.

The head is widely talked about in dozens of stroke recovery books that nail down the nitty gritty details of the brain and body. These books are essential for their technical information, but they're all missing something:

Love – the element that makes everything fall into place.

From the start, you should know that this isn't your average stroke recovery book. Instead of focusing on your muscles, I'm going to focus on your mindset. We're going to clear away all the inner blocks that are preventing you from approaching your recovery – and yourself – with love.

This begs the question, "Why does stroke recovery need love? Isn't it just about getting your body back to the way it was before?" Well, sure... in a way. But recovering from stroke is a long, hard process. One that takes time and patience. And without cultivating a solid foundation within yourself first, the rest cannot follow – or it will follow with difficulty.

Your body and brain take the shape of your beliefs. If you don't believe in yourself, you'll attempt to force and shame yourself to get back to where you were before – and it's a hard-won battle. A better way includes much less fear and far more love. And in order to love yourself, you need to *know yourself*.

Beginning the Process

Part of self-knowledge comes from understanding your own values and how they shape who you are and how you deal with the world around you. Another part comes from gaining awareness of your brain mechanics and psychology, which both influence your mind and create your predispositions.

By simply becoming aware of these parts of yourself, you enter into a more loving phase in your life. This book will help you get there. Here's a brief outline of what's in store.

First, we will cover the basics of how your brain heals after stroke. Specifically, we will explore the phenomenon of neuroplasticity, which is the process that your brain uses to rewire itself and create new mental traits.

You will see references to neuroplasticity sprinkled all throughout this book. Neuroplasticity is a central concept because it can be applied to much more than healing – it can be applied to happiness, too.

Then we will move onto beliefs. Our beliefs shape our future because they guide our actions. If we have limiting beliefs stuck in our psyche, then they will prevent us from taking the necessary action to achieve an amazing recovery – and everyone has the potential to achieve an amazing recovery!

After we uncover our beliefs, we will dig deeper into our psychology by addressing emotions. Once you understand exactly where your emotions are coming from, you can start to move past the negative emotions and cultivate more positive ones.

Next, we will dig into the most personal part of stroke recovery: identity and self-esteem. You will learn why your sense of identity could be suffering after stroke and, more importantly, how to rebuild it. Then you'll learn the most essential tool for boosting self-esteem: the Framework.

From there, we will cover all the extra tidbits that can make a good recovery great. We will discuss how to develop motivation, overcome fear, and boost happiness. Once you have the fundamentals in place, these tips will take you the extra mile.

Finally, you will learn about self-acceptance and self-love, the two most essential elements for healing and happiness.

As you continue to read, I'll take you chapter by chapter through each of the steps outlined above. Starting with Chapter 3, you will find Exercises and Essential Habits in each chapter (usually at the end), and I encourage you to try them all. You may want to read the book once all the way through, and then go back and try the exercises. Or, you may want to focus on one chapter at a time until you have all the ideas, exercises, and habits for that chapter mastered. Do whatever works best for you.

Now get ready. Learning how to love yourself takes relentless awareness and self-understanding, and that's what this book is all about. You will learn the tools to get back up and start life anew.

It all starts with the brain and ends with the heart.

Chapter 2
Healing the Brain

"If you are persistent, you will get it.
If you are consistent, you will keep it."

–Unknown

A large part of self-understanding comes from under-standing your psychology, the mechanics of your *mind* that influence everything you think, feel, and do. But before diving in, it's important to note that your mind is very different from your brain.

To distinguish, your *brain* consists of three pounds of tissue in your skull that executes mental and physical tasks. Consider it your tangible hardware (like a desktop computer).

Your *mind* is like your intangible software (like Microsoft Word) that includes all the beliefs, thoughts, and feelings that you can't see. However, this software significantly influences the physical tasks that your brain executes.

During stroke recovery, it is possible – and necessary – to work on both your brain and your mind at once.

Most of this book is concerned with matters of the mind. But we need to cover one fundamental concept about the brain first: neuroplasticity, the mechanism that can heal your brain and, surprisingly, every other aspect of your life, too.

Your Chameleon Brain

Scientists once thought that the brain was incapable of change. They said, "These are the different parts of the brain, this is what each part controls, and that's it!" Easy. Done.

Except it wasn't done. Early science got it wrong.

In the mid-1900's researchers realized that the brain isn't nearly as rigid as they once thought. In fact, the brain is capable of changing itself based solely on *what you want* to change. Talk about personal empowerment!

You want to learn a new language? Become an elite athlete? Recover from a stroke? If you focus on it every day – and if you want it bad enough – then your brain will adapt to meet your needs. *Your brain is a chameleon to your focus, molding and shaping itself to whatever skills you repetitively practice.*

Every time you repeat a pattern, the engaged area of your brain becomes stronger. In other words, whatever you obsessively focus on, that's what you get good at.

This phenomenon is known as neuroplasticity, and it's the 'software upgrade' that will help you become stronger after stroke. In theory it's simple. However, applying the theory takes hard work, dedication, and repetition. And your brain is on your side.

How Your Brain Changes Itself

To understand how neuroplasticity works, you need to know how the brain is wired, how it was disrupted, and how it can rewire itself again.

Consider for a moment that the brain is a large city full of interconnected highways and busy little people. These little people are the messages your brain uses to share information and control your muscles, and the highways are neurons, which allow these messages to travel to various parts of your body.

When a stroke damages part of the brain, it shuts down a large chunk of those highways and restricts access to important information. Suddenly, there's a big hole in the city and your brain's messages can't get where they need to go. As a result, you become stuck.

Luckily your brain has a mechanism to get unstuck. To get around the restricted highways, your brain will construct new roads. Neuroplasticity to the rescue!

How, you ask? Well, imagine that each of the little people in your brain (the messages that your brain is trying to send) are carrying a brick with them. When they reach a damaged highway, they find another route. An unpaved road.

At first, it is very difficult to travel on this road. But as they travel that uneven terrain, each person places their brick on the ground to make it easier for the next person that comes along.

In other words, the messages that your brain sends are also builders. Not only are they traveling along the old highways that already existed, but they are also creating new highways to get where they need to go!

In this way, neuroplasticity allows your brain to rewire itself and reconstruct new highways around the old, broken ones. Your brain learns how to send messages along these new neurons and regain access to the information it needs to communicate with your body.

There's a problem though: the people in this city only have one brick each. That means that in order to build a new highway, your brain has to send thousands and thousands of messages down the new roads.

It will be hard at first, but each new message will add another brick. Then as you relentlessly follow through again and again, the unpaved road will turn into a cobblestone path. And as your new foundation continues to strengthen, it will finally become the express highway you need.

This process is called repetitive practice, and it's how you'll achieve an amazing recovery.

Maximize Your Recovery with Repetitive Practice

After a stroke, the communication between your brain and your muscles has become damaged, typically on one side of the body. To compensate for this, some survivors tend to ignore their affected side and focus all attention on their unaffected muscles. But this is the exact opposite of what you need to do.

When you focus your attention on your affected muscles, your brain will notice the problem and adapt to meet your needs. But this only works if you focus on the problem repetitively.

Isn't that how you would respond too?

If something only bothered you once, like your car's single ding for an oil change, you probably wouldn't go out of your way to fix it. But if it kept bugging you over and over again, you'd be much more inclined to address the problem.

That's exactly how your brain works. For example, if you want to regain hand function, you have to start by bringing attention into your affected hand. Then you have to practice hand exercises over and over, day in and day out.

Repetitive practice let's your brain know that there's a problem that you really want to fix, and it will adapt to meet your needs. Then with lots of time and effort, your brain will rewire itself to regain more function and control.

If this sounds daunting, don't be discouraged. I know a stroke survivor who could only stand on his affected leg for two or three seconds when he began rehabilitation. After his first week of repetitive practice, he could stand on his affected leg for six seconds. Then, after two more weeks of repetitive practice, it was ten seconds. The progress was slow, but it was steady.

Eventually he regained the full ability to walk, which is a clear example of the brain reconstructing new highways. It's proof that repetitive practice works.

Together, neuroplasticity and repetitive practice are how your brain heals during stroke recovery. There are many other important factors that go into a healthy, safe recovery, but these are your bread and butter. Get them lined up and you're in great shape.

However, your brain is just the hardware. You need to address your mind's software too if you want to improve in all areas – and that's why your psychology matters so much. As you get your brain in order, you also have the opportunity to get your mind in order as well. This is where the phrase 'stronger after stroke' really comes into play.

Chapter 3
Revealing the Truth

"Whether you think you can, or you think
you can't – you're right."

–Henry Ford

Your psychology begins with your beliefs, which are mental patterns that influence the way you view the world. Whenever you receive new information, it gets sifted through the filter of your beliefs.

If your beliefs are limited, then your thoughts, feelings, and actions will also be limited. The good news is that the opposite is also true. If you can free your beliefs, you can free your potential. You can turn your thoughts, feelings, and actions into something that propels you forward instead of holding you back.

The Language of Truth

"Don't ever let anyone tell you, you can't do something."

–Will Smith (The Pursuit of Happiness)

Now, this may come as a shock to some, but you probably haven't heard the full truth about stroke recovery. At least not with the correct *language*, and the language someone uses to discuss your future has an *immense* impact on your beliefs.

For example, if someone told you that you can't achieve a full recovery, it will have an effect on you. Whether you believe it or not, it becomes part of that little nagging voice in your head that says you can't do it.

The people in our lives don't mean to impose limiting beliefs on us. Doctors, therapists, friends, and family all have pure intentions, but they may not understand what actually happens to your psychology when they tell you that you can't do something.

This unintentional limiting happens all the time during stroke recovery. Limiting beliefs can creep in when discussing plateaus in your progress, the possible extent of your recovery, and the purpose of your compensation techniques. You may have been misguided in some of these areas, and together we're going to set things straight.

So prepare for this unraveling. Prepare to take all the limiting beliefs you have, crumple them into a ball, and toss them into the garbage.

You won't need them anymore.

Limiting Belief #1:
The Plateau

When survivors hit a plateau during physical therapy, results start to slow down and may no longer be measurable over short time periods. At this point, insurance typically stops coverage and therapists are likely to discharge patients for the sake of saving the patients money.

The miscommunication occurs when the patient thinks that the end of 'measurable results' means the end of recovery. That is simply *not* the case. The plateau is not the end of recovery, it's simply the end of a 'heightened state of plasticity.'[1]

This refers to a phase that occurs right after stroke where neuroplasticity intensifies as the brain rapidly tries to heal itself, typically causing noticeable improvement in the first few months of recovery. After this phase, the rate of neuroplasticity slows down, creating the illusion of a plateau. But the brain will never stop trying to heal and improve itself.

Neuroplasticity works wherever we put in the effort.

Recovery only stops when you stop.

A good tip to pull yourself out of a plateau is to add variety and challenge to your regimen. You need to shake things up so that your brain gets the stimulation it needs to rewire. As you continue to progress and try different forms of therapy, you will continue to get better.

There will be times when you move forward and times when you go backwards. Don't let yourself be discouraged by a bad day or week. Remind yourself that when you zoom out and look at the bigger picture, there's always a trend of upward growth.

Small signs of improvement should always be celebrated. There will be an exercise to reinforce this at the end of the chapter.

Limiting Belief #2:
You Can't Achieve a Full Recovery

What makes the difference between those who can achieve a full recovery and those who can't? Severity of the stroke and available resources are two huge factors, but there's one thing that everyone has the equal opportunity to tap into: your mindset – the ability to reject limiting beliefs and create your own story.

If, for whatever reason, someone else told you that you'll be stuck in a wheelchair forever, or that you'll never be able to use your arm again, or that you'll only be able to [insert your fate here], then they are trying to put you under the influence of *their* limiting beliefs.

Whether or not you buy into them is *your* choice.

Your beliefs influence your actions, which in turn reinforce your limiting beliefs even more. This continuous cycle can either heal you or harm you. For example, if you don't believe that a full recovery is possible, then you you're unlikely to try to get there. As a consequence, your inaction guarantees that you won't make any progress because recovery requires repetitive practice.

This only further reinforces your limiting belief since you will feel like you aren't getting any better, just like you thought! In psychology this is known as a self-fulfilling prophecy, where the story becomes true simply because of the very story itself.

So, if you're feeling trapped by the limitations of your recovery, then start to become mindful of the story you tell yourself. Recognize any limiting beliefs you have and turn them around. Create a narrative that supports you instead of hinders you.

For example, right before giving a speech in front of a large audience, you wouldn't tell yourself, "I can't do this. I'm a horrible public speaker, and there's no way I can remember everything." If you told yourself that story, then you're guaranteed to choke.

When you switch the narrative around and think, "I've rehearsed this speech dozens of times, and I'm confident that I can deliver it smoothly," then you'll do much better than the former example. The encouraging thoughts will improve your performance and create an upward spiral of positive beliefs that inspire positive action.

You can take this same powerful approach with your recovery, and Chapter 6 will show you how.

Limiting Belief #3:
Compensation Techniques are the End

Our brain has a built-in, biological mechanism to constantly remain on the lookout for shortcuts that save us time and energy. A good stroke recovery, however, requires that you override that impulse.

Working towards doing things *without* shortcuts – commonly referred to as compensation techniques – is the only way to maximize movement recovery after stroke. This raises the question, how does compensation differ from recovery?

Compensation involves performing an old movement in a new manner. *Recovery* involves restoring the ability to move in the same manner as before. For example, making a sandwich with one hand is compensation. Making a sandwich with both hands, despite how slow and frustrating it can be, is recovery. When possible, you always want to choose recovery over compensation.

Please understand that compensation techniques are not always bad, especially in the beginning stages of stroke recovery when you can't get around without them. However, as you continue to improve, you may regain the ability to move without using your compensation techniques. However, you won't realize that you can until you try to live without them.

Mindfulness becomes extremely important during this stage. As you progress through your recovery, constantly ask yourself whether your compensation techniques are necessary, or simply convenient. If they're necessary, keep at it. If they're convenient, then you have a choice to make: stay in comfort or move into growth.

Your biological instinct will tell you to stay in comfort because compensation saves you time and energy. But it won't get you to an amazing recovery. You need to use your affected muscles in order to regain control of them, and this means doing things the hard – yet rewarding – way.

Your ability to choose growth will fluctuate from day to day, so always keep your ultimate, long-term goal in mind: a full recovery free of compensation. There will be days where you have zero patience to exercise your affected muscles, and there will be days when you are fully motivated.

You win when you can take advantage of the days when you feel good and avoid shaming yourself on the days when you don't.

Curiosity Makes the Difference

Curiosity can serve you well in stroke recovery.

You can only find freedom by identifying your limiting beliefs first, and then working on releasing them. The process starts with awareness, which can be cultivated through *self-inquiry*. There will be an exercise on self-inquiry at the end of this chapter to help you master this integral step.

As a general overview, self-inquiry starts by looking at your life and recovery process to see if you can find any particular places where you feel stuck. You must become aware of how they're limiting your recovery, and then *question the heck out of them*.

Was your doctor wrong about your potential? Can you get yourself to walk again? Can you recover just a little bit more?

Can you achieve a full recovery?

The answer to these questions may not always be yes, but you won't know unless you ask.

I once met a stroke survivor with partial hand movement who decided that he wanted to get his hand back – *24 years post-stroke*. His family members didn't think it was possible so 'late in the game,' but he rejected their limiting beliefs and took matters into his own hands.

He was ambitious, yes. But I would argue that he was more curious than anything. All he wanted was to see how far he could go. So he researched his options, dedicated himself to a new, innovative regimen, and regained his hand function! It wasn't easy or quick, but he got there.

And it all started with a little curiosity.

Exercise: Keep a Success Journal

"Whenever you find yourself doubting how far you can go, just remember how far you have come. Remember everything you have faced, all the battles you have won, and all the fears you have overcome."

–Unknown

A success journal is a great way to celebrate all the tiny accomplishments during recovery that deserve celebration. By keeping a written record of them, you can focus on what you're doing right. This will help generate self-esteem while retraining your brain to look for what's going right in our lives.

A success journal will help you cherish your tiny improvements so that you can see how far you've come and generate a sense of well-deserved accomplishment. It will also keep you on the lookout for things to celebrate and love all day long, which is a great way to live.

So take some time right now to write down 3 big successes that you've had since your stroke. Then write down 10 small successes you've had this week. If you don't think you've had 10 successes, think again.

Some examples of tiny successes are: starting a new exercise regimen; getting all the way through an exercise; writing in your stroke recovery journal; getting ready in the morning; meditating for two minutes; getting ready a little faster this morning; taking a bite with your affected hand; cooking with your affected hand; a little more movement in your leg; feeling more patient with your family today; feeling more patient with the world today.

The list goes on and on – and I encourage you to allow it to go on and on! You don't have to stop at ten. If you can find more, keep going. Every single tiny thing should be celebrated.

And whenever you're feeling down or unmotivated, go back and reread your successes. It will make you feel better about how far you've come and restore your sense of progress and confidence in your growing abilities.

Exercise: Self-Inquiry

Self-inquiry is the best way to become aware of your beliefs. This is important because sometimes we carry around limiting beliefs without even knowing it!

For those who are new to this concept, self-inquiry is the process of entering dialogue with yourself, where you can discover more than 'thinking in your head' could ever allow. Through self-inquiry, you can discover where your beliefs are limiting you, which will show you the exact areas that need to be rewired.

So, for this guided self-inquiry, start by identifying any limiting beliefs you have about your recovery and write them down on paper. If writing is not for you, you can also say them out loud into a voice recorder. The important thing is to *avoid doing this exercise only in your head.* If you do, then your own unconscious biases will get in the way. Externalizing your beliefs separates you from that mechanism.

Once you have identified your limiting beliefs and written them down or recorded them, go through each of them and answer these three questions:

Question 1: Is this belief absolutely, 100% true?

In other words, can you prove this belief in a court of law? Sometimes our opinions feel true, but when you take a deep look at them, they're really just opinions. When answering this question, be very careful to make sure that you aren't confusing fact with fiction.

Question 2: How do you react with this belief in your life?

Your reactions can include the way you think, behave, feel, and live because of the belief. Here, pay attention to the self-talk that goes on inside your head and how that self-talk influences your behavior and emotions. Make a list of all your reactions and let the dialogue flow.

Question 3: How would you react *without* this belief?

In other words, what would you think, feel, and do differently?

This last question is the most important because this is where significant progress can be made. Often, our beliefs are the only thing standing in the way of what we want but *think* we can't have. Through this dialogue, you may realize where you're selling yourself short and where you have more room to grow.

To provide more context, here's an example self-inquiry performed on the belief of a limited recovery.

Question 1: Can you absolutely, 100% know that you'll never be able to achieve a full recovery?

If a doctor told you that you couldn't achieve a full recovery, then you may assume that it's a fact. But every stroke is different, which means every stroke recovery is different. And no doctor knows for *certain* that you will not be able to achieve a full recovery. Miracle stories are proof of this.

At this point, you may realize exactly how sneaky your thoughts can be when they disguise themselves as facts.

Question 2: How does the belief of a limited recovery make you react?

Here you realize that the belief in a limited recovery discourages you from exercising and exploring your options, and it drains your motivation and happiness. After this question, you may start to realize the consequences of carrying around this limiting belief.

Question 3: How would you react with the belief of a *full* recovery?

Finally, when you consider the idea of replacing the old limiting belief with a far more encouraging one, you start to realize your untapped potential. You realize that believing in a full recovery gives you a reason to start exercising again. You also find that it promotes far more happiness and hope than before.

By performing self-inquiry multiple times across any and all limiting beliefs, you will start to get a real sense of how your beliefs guide your feelings and actions. Through practice, you can develop a whole new way of thinking – one that will serve you and your recovery far better.

Essential Habit: Keep a Stroke Recovery Journal to Increase Self-Understanding

"The process of writing can be a powerful tool for self-discovery. Writing demands self-knowledge; it forces the writer to become a student of human nature, to pay attention to his experience, to understand the nature of experience itself."

–Georg Buehler

Revealing the Truth is about revealing yourself and your beliefs through self-inquiry and self-discovery. One of the best tools to continue this self-discovery long-term is a journal.

Sometimes *we don't know what we know until we write it down*, and a stroke recovery journal can help you realize important things about your recovery – like where you're accidentally limiting yourself, where you could improve, and how far you've come. Years down the line, you'll be able to look back and appreciate how far you've come and remember all the lessons you've learned.

So find a notebook – a nice, fresh one that you find particularly inviting – and make a habit of writing in it every day for a minimum of one minute. Setting a goal of just one minute helps turn it into a habit because it's very doable. If you want to write more, please do. If not, you're still writing every day, which will help more than you realize.

I know a stroke survivor who wished that she had recorded her entire recovery in a journal. Even as a former writer, it took her *years* to realize the healing powers of journaling. Before she started the habit 5 years post-stroke, she felt like she was subconsciously storing all her troubles in her body. It wasn't until after she started journaling that she began to get it all out and finally sort through it.

So take her word for it and start your journal *today*. It doesn't matter what you write. If there's something that needs to be worked through, it will find its way into your journal.

And if you are unable to use your writing hand, then make a habit of talking into a voice recorder. It may feel silly, but it's just as therapeutic as writing in a journal – and it's faster, too.

Whatever you choose, do yourself the favor of writing or talking about your recovery daily. It will reveal far more truth than you could ever anticipate.

Chapter 4
Navigating New Emotions

"If you want peace, stop fighting.
If you want peace of mind,
stop fighting with your thoughts."

–Peter McWilliams

Once limiting beliefs are out of the way, you've already advanced farther than most. The next step in the healing process is to understand and manage your emotions – specifically negative emotions like grief and anger.

Emotions deserve special attention because they are typically overlooked during stroke recovery. Unfortunately, they're often written off as a mere side effect of the brain injury. As if, once recovery is over, the emotions will go away. However, this is seldom the case.

Recovery is never 'over,' and waiting for something bad to end before something good can begin doesn't make much sense. By dealing with your negative emotions head on, you can start removing the barriers to happiness *now*.

You are not your stroke, and you are also not your emotions. As you work to free yourself from the limitations of both, it's critical to understand where those stuck feelings are coming from.

This chapter will guide you through the psychology of each negative emotion you may experience after stroke, and then provide you with tools to pull yourself out.

How to Use This Chapter

If you talk to any psychologist about emotions, they will tell you that all emotions are caused by *thoughts*. No emotion can exist without a thought behind it. And if that sounds crazy, you will learn about this phenomenon in detail in Chapter 6. For now, trust that the root of your emotions always lies within your thoughts.

During stroke recovery, however, there is a wild exception to this: emotional lability, which occurs when there is damage to the emotion center of the brain (more on this in the next section). This creates a *physical* incapability – not just a mental one to control your emotions. Since the brain is still healing, a common mistake among those who suffer from emotional lability is trying to strong-arm their emotions, which only leads to defeat and exhaustion.

Therefore, if you suffer from emotional lability, the tools in this chapter can help but they may not have maximum impact until the lability is a bit more under control. By familiarizing yourself with the tools now, you can start practicing them early. That way, when your lability does settle down, you will know exactly how to tend to your emotions.

Aside from those with emotional lability, there are two other general groups of stroke survivors: those who deal with many negative emotions and those who do not. If you're someone who does not deal with negative emotions on a daily basis, then this section may not resonate with you – and that's great. It means you have one less obstacle to overcome. However, since negative emotions are unavoidable – after all, suffering is part of our shared humanity and we all experience it – you may still find this chapter useful.

For the final group — those who deal with negative emotions on a daily basis — this chapter is essential. All the new problems and life situations that come with stroke recovery can intensify negative thoughts and emotions, and this chapter will show you to work through it.

If you find that some sections resonate with you more than others, then you know where to focus your attention. Remember to avoid beating yourself up over any of your emotions. Suffering is unavoidable, but not unmanageable. You are on the road to recovery, and you will come out with a deeper understanding of yourself and an improved ability to manage life's hardships.

Emotional Lability (Uncontrollable Emotions)

Emotional lability is caused by damage in the emotion center of the brain. As a result, the condition can trigger random outbursts of emotion or make normal reactions more intense. You may find yourself hysterically laughing at something that isn't nearly funny or crying for no apparent reason.

Emotional lability is a medically diagnosed condition, and unfortunately many stroke survivors go undiagnosed. However, instead of fixating on the cause of uncontrollable emotions, it's best to focus all your effort into practicing self-compassion. Whatever emotions bubble up, try not to judge yourself or allow yourself to feel judged by others. When emotional outbursts happen, let it flow, and try to have a sense of humor about it when possible.

If you laugh at spilled milk, then laugh at spilled milk. If you cry for no apparent reason, then let yourself cry.

There's a world of difference between wishing these emotions didn't happen and just letting them flow. The key is to allow yourself to experience them without resisting the discomfort. You'll release them much faster this way.

Now, you don't have to do all this hard work alone. In fact, there are ways to gather the support you need to make the process easier on yourself.

For example, when outbursts happen around family or friends, keep them clued in on what's happening to help avoid any misunderstandings or hurt feelings. Let them know that you might have emotional lability as a result of your stroke, and they will be much more understanding and supportive.

Before you do this, however, take some time to decide how you want to be treated when you have outbursts. Do you want others to pretend like nothing happened? Do you want them to address each episode? Would you feel comforted by a simple hug, or do you need space?

What would make you feel the most supported and cared for?

Sometimes we don't know what we want until we sit down and give it some thought. This step is particularly important because if *you* don't know how you wanted to be treated, then others probably have no idea either.

By figuring yourself out first and communicating your desires to your loved ones, they will be far more willing and able to comfort you during difficult times. They will appreciate your guidance, and you will benefit from it too.

Practicing Self-Compassion

As you work through all difficult emotions – especially emotional lability – it's essential to practice self-compassion as much as possible. In order to understand what self-compassion really means, it helps to look at what compassion with *others* means first.

When you feel compassion for others, you probably take care of them. And when you see them suffer, you probably try to make them feel better through warm, caring words and actions. This type of kindness is compassion.

To exercise *self*-compassion means treating yourself with the same warm, caring behavior that you exercise towards others. It means talking kindly to yourself and being gentle with yourself, especially when things are tough.

Whenever you notice a negative feeling, treat it as the perfect opportunity to exercise self-compassion. Instead of criticizing yourself, speak kindly instead. Ask yourself, "What would I say to someone who was criticizing herself the same way as me? How would I comfort her?" Then comfort yourself in the same manner.

Dealing with Anxious Thoughts

Everyone deals with anxiety, but during stroke recovery the emotion can be exhausting. With so many unknown variables and new problems to solve, your brain naturally turns on its *problem-solving mode* – and stays there. (This will be discussed in detail in Chapter 9.) The resulting mindset causes you to focus on the worst case scenario, which only pushes you deeper into anxiety.

While the emotion may feel totally out of control, you always have the ability to control your thoughts – and that's great news. It means that the key to working through anxiety, then, is to *choose different thoughts* than the ones that are keeping you stuck.

For example, if you continuously think about how long stroke recovery is going to take, then it's only going to perpetuate your anxiety. But if you shift your thoughts over to something more empowering, like how far you have come, then you take fuel away from your anxiety.

Therefore, the first step to help relieve anxiety is to cultivate awareness. Start by asking yourself, "What are the exact thoughts that are generating my anxiety?" Be as specific as you can, and then turn them around.

Although the solution sounds simple, applying it can prove quite difficult because anxious thoughts often occur subconsciously. The only way to make it easier is to practice, practice, practice. The *skill* of reversing anxious thoughts won't come all at once. Rather, a steady, focused effort towards generating awareness of anxious thoughts and turning them around will generate the results you want.

You will learn much more about this process in Chapter 6.

5 Stages of Grief

"The only way out is through."

–Robert Frost

Grief is a troubling emotion that often accompanies loss. During stroke recovery, grief can be triggered by losses such as the loss of function, the inability to work or participate in hobbies, or even the loss of one's self-perception as a healthy individual.

While working through grief, it's *especially* important to practice self-compassion at all times. While no one ever wants to go through grief, it's a process that must be honored. The only way out is through.

In my eyes, this is the biggest reason why survivors become stronger after stroke. Because if you can go through the uncomfortable process of navigating new emotions, then you will – *without a doubt* – become a stronger version of yourself.

This section will help you understand grief by discussing its five stages. You may not experience the stages in order, and you may even go back and forth between some stages until you can find acceptance – and this is normal.

Grief is not a linear process, and neither is your recovery.

Allow the ebb and flow of healing to run its course.

Stage 1: Shock

Shock typically occurs immediately after stroke. Questions may arise like, what happened? How? Surely not me? This stage is often fleeting, but sometimes it lingers. The best way to cope with shock is simply with the passage of time.

Stage 2: Anger

Anger is never pretty, and learning how to deal with it appropriately can help us avoid the side effects of unruly emotional expression. The best way to manage anger is by understanding the psychological triggers, which can be boiled down into two root causes: 1) trying to control something you can't control and 2) trying to impose your values on someone else.

First, let's talk about control. The only thing we ever have control over is our thoughts. We can attempt to control our body, careers, relationships, nurses, and everyone and everything else in our lives, but curveballs are inevitable.

And when we attempt to control something that we can't control, we set ourselves up for failure. At the end of the day, life happens the way it happens and people behave the way they want to behave. Expecting anything else is self-defeating.

Therefore, we must let go of our outer expectations in order to end feelings of anger. This can be challenging because we often feel very justified in our anger. The thoughts go something along the lines of, "But this person did this; but that person said that; but my body did this and won't do that; etc."

As you can see, this puts us in a state of blame, which is a disempowering place to be. We want to avoid blame as much as possible.

The solution to anger is to move from blame to acceptance. By reminding ourselves that anger is only caused by thoughts, it can help restore our personal power. When we accept the things we cannot control, we can start creating better thoughts that lead to less anger and more happiness.

The second major cause of anger is trying to impose our *values* on someone else. We all have values that we hold close to our hearts, and we feel great when we're living in alignment with them. (There is an exercise for identifying your values at the end of Chapter 5.)

When we fail to uphold our values, however, we feel pain. And when *other people* fail to uphold *our own* values, we feel anger.

When we expect other people to behave according to our own values (no matter how much sense it would make), we're once again trying to control something we can't control. Everyone is their own unique person and carries their own unique values. We can't expect them to uphold our values too – that's our job.

The next time you feel angry with someone, try adding a second layer to your self-inquiry by asking yourself how their actions don't agree with your values. We can usually spot this problem when we find ourselves saying the words, *"I wouldn't have..."*

For example, "I wouldn't have treated someone that way," or "I wouldn't have said that," or "I wouldn't have done that thing you just did." When we say those words, we're blaming the other person using the measuring stick of our own personal values. And a healthier goal is to learn to accept the situation and remain empowered.

So, instead of resorting to blame, try to flip the situation around. Instead of trying to impose your values on someone else, use that energy to strengthen your own values instead, like patience, compassion, or empathy. As an added benefit, this can even make you grateful for the particularly aggravating people in your life, since they are giving you the most opportunities to practice!

As with all things, this requires patience. Each time you feel yourself getting angry, stop and ask yourself why. Walk away if you need to. Figure out the specific thoughts that are creating your anger, and then make the choice to turn them around.

Stage 3: Bargaining

Those who feel particularly out of control during stroke recovery may use bargaining as a grieving mechanism. Bargaining includes personal if/then promises to a higher power. For example, a bargainer may find themselves saying, "If I go to rehab every day this week without fail, then please let this spasticity go away."

Bargaining is a step in both the right and wrong direction.

Bargaining shows that you're willing and motivated to do something, but you expect something in return – which isn't always ideal. Because when you place your motivation outside of yourself, you risk losing your motivation when you don't achieve your desired results.

If your spasticity doesn't go away, then what?

Will you keep going anyway?

Keep a close eye on where you place your motivation, and always try to place it within yourself. When you give your recovery everything you have and expect nothing in return, amazing things happen. You won't get derailed if you don't see the results you wanted, and you end up achieving much more in the long run.

Stage 4: Depression

There are many different causes for post-stroke depression, like the mourning of a life once had, low self-esteem, the biochemical impact of your stroke, lack of support, and shame. It's a heart-wrenching reality, but there is hope. Let's discuss each cause.

Mourning of a Life Once Had

When post-stroke side effects take away your ability to live and behave like before, the differences between your life before and after stroke can cause grief and depression. Addressing your identity is a great way to alleviate this type of post-stroke depression, and we will discuss that in detail in the next chapter.

Low Self-Esteem

Low self-esteem can also contribute to post-stroke depression. When your self-image takes a toll after stroke, then learning how to feel good about yourself should be a top priority. Chapter 6 is dedicated explicitly to this.

Biochemical Impact of Your Stroke

The biochemical impact of your stroke can be a surprising cause of post-stroke depression. To understand why, let's take a look at the two main sources of happiness.

Happiness is influenced by both your psychology and your brain chemicals like dopamine, oxytocin, serotonin, and endorphins – also known as 'happiness chemicals.'

If your stroke reduced your brain's ability to create these happiness chemicals, then it's important not to shrug off your depression as a side effect that you can beat by 'toughening up.'

You cannot control your biochemistry, and it's important not to blame yourself for something you cannot control.

The purpose of this book is to boost your happiness after stroke by addressing your psychology. If you try all the exercises in this book and nothing seems to help, then your depression might be the result of biochemical changes in your brain.

If you think that you suffer from this type of depression after stroke, then it's important that you talk to your doctor. They may be able to suggest a treatment that can help.

Lack of Support

Lack of support can also cause post-stroke depression due to our deeply rooted need for human connection. Support is absolutely vital during tough, vulnerable times like stroke recovery.

If you can't find the support you need from family and friends, then try to find a stroke support group in your area. The American Stroke Association has a support group finder on their website that you can use.

If there aren't any support groups in your area, then you can join an online stroke support group. (For example, you can find a link to Flint Rehab's online stroke support group on their website.)

Stroke survivors who participate in online groups find great joy in their ability to connect with others who are also recovering from stroke – even if they are on the other side of the world!

There are many options. Choose what is most comfortable to you.

Shame

Finally, post-stroke depression can also be caused by shame, which often makes us feel unloveable, lacking, and not enough. When left unaddressed, these feelings can lead to depression and isolation.

If you feel like you struggle with your sense of worth, then overcoming shame could be your key to happiness. There is a section in the last chapter of this book that will show you the steps to get there.

This is by no means a complete list of the causes of post-stroke depression. So please don't worry if this section doesn't give you an *a-ha* moment. This *whole book* is geared towards relieving post-stroke depression. Factors like reestablishing your identity, boosting self-esteem, obliterating limiting beliefs, practicing self-acceptance, and learning how to love yourself are all *monumental* in relieving post-stroke depression.

You're on the right track!

Stage 5: Acceptance

Once you move through your own unique grieving process, you can enter the final stage: self-acceptance. For many, self-acceptance is not an easy stage to reach. It requires lots of uncomfortable time spent looking deep within yourself to figure out exactly where your pain is coming from.

Although the road towards self-acceptance can be painful, it's also full of self-discovery. You'll learn how to create the changes and results that you want to see; and you'll learn to always start from within.

Exercise: Write Yourself a Compassionate Letter

When we fall into negative emotions, our self-criticism tends to run rampant. To calm down your inner critic during distressing times, try writing a compassionate letter to yourself. And if you don't have the ability to write yet, you can do this exercise with a voice recorder.

First, take time to identify exactly what's causing your emotions. Are you worried about something in the future? Are you feeling insecure about your recovery or your body? Where is your pain coming from?

Then, write a letter to yourself from the perspective of a caring friend.

How would they convey their compassion towards the pain you feel? What would they say about your pain from the perspective of unlimited compassion? What changes would they suggest you make to your thinking and/or life?

As you write the letter, try to use *exclusively* loving, kind, and caring words – things that only a loving friend would use.

When you're done writing your letter, read it through and allow the compassion to pour into you. Then put it down for a little while and come back to it later and read it *again*, and really let it sink in this time.

Then, if you ever feel yourself suffering from the same pain again, reread your letter. Or, if the writing process is therapeutic to you, write a new one. There's no such thing as too many self-love notes.

Essential Habit: Have Practice Periods to Increase Your Patience

When dealing with negative emotions, a great skill to develop is patience. Having patience with yourself and others will help you take things less personally and prepare for the long road to recovery ahead. And like all skills, patience is one that can be cultivated through intentional practice.

For this habit, pick 20 minutes a day to practice patience. If possible, you want to try this when you're interacting with other people or sitting in waiting rooms. During these 20 minutes, be extra patient with everything. Allow things to take longer than they need to, allow people to do what they want to do, and allow yourself to be patient with all of it.

Celebrate the slowness of life.

By doing this for 20 minutes every day, you will train your brain to be more patient. With enough practice, you will notice that it's much easier to be patient even when you aren't having your 'practice periods.'

Chapter 5
Reestablishing Your Identity

"He who has a why to live for

can bear almost any how."

−Friedrich Nietzsche

In the previous chapter, I mentioned that the differences between life before and after stroke can cause depression − and now we're going to work through that problem.

Identity-related depression usually happens when post-stroke side effects take away your ability to live and behave like before. This can be especially painful if you still strongly identify with your previous lifestyle.

For example, most body builders and triathletes heavily identify with their athletic ability. It's their source of happiness. And there's absolutely nothing wrong with this − until their ability to move is compromised. And if their disability is severe, it would create a startling gap in their identity and happiness.

As a result, the disconnection between their past and present creates a stressful urgency to get back to life as it was before. If you can relate to this, then it means that you heavily identify with your life before stroke.

Again, there is absolutely nothing wrong with this – until it causes you to delay your happiness until you get your old life back. *You should never delay your happiness.* You deserve to feel happy *during* your recovery instead of waiting until the destination.

Therefore, to start creating happiness *now*, you can try bridging the gap between your *abilities* and your *desires*. This means that you can either 1) change *what* you do, or 2) change the reason *why* you do it. Through this process, you'll learn how to add more purpose and meaning to your life, which will help restore your sense of identity.

Your Ultimate Life

Your sense of identity is closely tied to your vision of the Ultimate Life, which includes the deep passions and desires that you dreamt of as a kid or developed affinity for along the way. It includes the expectations of what you hope to become and achieve in the grand scheme of your life.

Your Ultimate Life could involve sophisticated goals such as becoming a world traveler or entrepreneur. Or, it could simply involve making a modest living, retiring at 65, and playing golf into your late days.

Everyone has their own unique vision of the Ultimate Life, and you will feel the most complete when you're either living it or making progress towards getting there.

When your ability to pursue your Ultimate Life is taken away, you may feel incomplete. This can create emotional pain, tarnish your self-esteem, and further diminish your sense of self.

However, there's a way to restore your sense of identity. The first method involves *progress*, and the second method involves *change*.

Making Progress

When we feel like we've lost ourselves, we can restore part of that loss through progress. Because when we make progress towards reclaiming our life, we feel empowered. Progress is growth, and as long as we're growing, we feel like our dreams are within reach. And even if those dreams are a long way off, progress can make us just as happy.

So, whatever you need in order to feel like *you* again, start taking small actions to get there. It doesn't matter how long it will take because you'll quickly start to feel better through the feeling of progress, not the ultimate success. That success just becomes the cherry on top.

For example, let's say that your Ultimate Life involves dancing. Specifically, you dream of owning your own dance studio and becoming famous one day. Before stroke, you were right on track to achieve that dream, and you were happy, whole, and fulfilled. Then, when stroke took away your ability to dance, it diminished your sense of identity. You were devastated that you couldn't pursue the art you loved anymore and it pushed you into depression.

However, you recently started going to outpatient therapy and have slowly started to work towards getting your life back again. The little inches of progress that you see are restoring hope that you can dance again and get your Ultimate Life back.

The more you work and improve, the better you feel. This is because you're making progress towards your Ultimate Life. Instead of waiting, you're taking control of your progress – and that's the best thing you can do for your sense of identity.

Now, if you feel like progress doesn't do much for you or is too slow and frustrating, then the next section is for you.

Making Changes

The second method of restoring your identity involves *change*. First, take some time during the next few days or weeks to reflect on what type of person you would be proud to become.

What sort of values would you like to see yourself upholding? What do you hope to contribute to the world? What type of lifestyle would create the most meaning for you?

Then ask yourself, *why?*

Why do you want these things?

Once you dig deep down into the *root* of your desires, you'll find your values. These can be things like honesty, determination, self-esteem, love, patience, etc. Whatever they are, you will find that your values have everything to do with your sense of self.

You will also notice that your values aren't tied to your abilities. Rather, they're tied to your sense of *growth, contribution, and fulfillment* – and that's the best news of all. It means that you don't need to get your abilities back in order to live a fulfilling life. You just need to find a different outlet for the time being.

Perhaps you once dreamed of becoming a public speaker. If stroke left you with aphasia, then it would seem like your dreams are lost – but far from it! If you dig into your root desire, you may find that speaking isn't the most important factor. Rather, your true desire was to inspire other people.

Through this realization you realize that you don't need public speaking in order to inspire others and feel whole again. Instead, you can choose to volunteer at a charity that's meaningful to you and inspire people with your actions. It fulfills your purpose and keeps your values intact – and that's what matters most.

Bridging the Gap

As you can see, when your values are pure, you can always find a way to live your Ultimate Life, no matter the obstacles. It simply becomes a matter of bridging the gap between your *abilities* and your *desires*.

To reestablish your identity, you can either wait until your abilities catch up to your desires, or you can change your desires to reflect your abilities. Changing your abilities requires great time and effort. Changing your desires requires personal reflection and understanding.

From what I've seen, it works best to change your desires first, and then work on your abilities second. But it all depends on what your story is and what will make you happier long term.

Choosing to overcome aphasia in order to become a public speaker is an example of working on your abilities while keeping your desires the same. If you have the work ethic and patience to do something like this, then keep it up! However, sometimes we grow unhappy and stressed out while forcing ourselves back onto an old path.

Although persistence towards your goals is an admirable trait, it's important to know when to take a different direction. By giving less weight to *what* you want to do and focusing more on *why* you want to do it, you can keep your purpose and sense of identity alive.

And, in the future, you can always change your desires again to suit your growth.

You Are Exactly Where You Need to Be

If you find yourself resisting the idea of changing your desires, then a shift in perspective could be exactly what you need. Because in today's society, we have more control than ever before and we often like to think that we know exactly where we're headed.

But the truth is that we never *really* know how things are supposed to play out. Sometimes the most unfortunate circumstances are the greatest blessings in disguise – we just have to know how to look for those blessings. They rarely pop out and make themselves known. Instead, we have to dig deep within ourselves to uncover them.

For example, I know a middle-aged female who was a successful businesswoman before her stroke, and she was very proud of how high she had climbed the corporate ladder. Her success and reputation had become part of her identity.

When she suffered a stroke, it forced her to stop working, and it shattered her sense of self. She was devastated, but she quickly learned that it was the wake-up call she needed.

Her stroke forced her to slow down, which, of course, she hated at first. She questioned, "Why me? How long is this going to take? When will I be able to work again?"

She was filled with anguish as her recovery left her bedridden and she watched her colleague fill her position, and there was nothing she could do about it. She resisted her situation, and it only perpetuated the pain. But eventually she found the lesson within.

As her family began caring for her, she noticed that they felt like strangers – and it was the first time in *five years* that she realized it. She was shocked by this revelation. How could she have let herself neglect her family? *How long had this been happening?*

Through these questions she realized that, instead of building resentment towards her stroke, it was the perfect opportunity to reestablish her connection with her family. As her primary caretakers, she got to spend more time with them during the first 2 months of her recovery than she had in the previous five years!

And the best part was that once she recovered enough mobility to resume working, she decided to leave her old job for a new one with less hours and less glory – which didn't matter because it meant much more freedom. It allowed her to spend more time at home with her new priority: the people she loved.

I hope this story can serve as a reminder that, although we cannot see it sometimes, we are always exactly where we need to be. And when we can't see it, we need to have faith that every obstacle is here to serve a purpose and shape us into stronger versions of ourselves.

Exercise: Identifying Your Values

By now, you should be convinced that in order to reestablish your identity, you need to understand your values because they will give you something everlasting in which to ground your sense of self. However, we often don't know what our values are until we reason through it and write them down, and this exercise will help with that.

Step 1: Using the following table (or draw one of your own), write down the following:

- Your 3 greatest moments of accomplishment
- Your 3 greatest moments of happiness
- Your 3 greatest moments of failure

Step 2: Then, for each category, try to identify any themes that emerge. What personal qualities led to your accomplishments? Do similar things make you happy? What do your past failures show that you need to work on?

Usually there will be common threads within each category.

Step 3: Write down a few sentences of advice that you would give yourself based on the trends that emerge. What can you do to replicate feelings of accomplishment and happiness? What can you work on to avoid repeating past failures?

Step 4: Boil your advice down into a handful of words. These words are your core values.

Important Moments		
3 Greatest Moments of Accomplishment	3 Greatest Moments of Happiness	3 Greatest Moments of Failure
1. 2. 3.	1. 2. 3.	1. 2. 3.
Themes		
Advice		
Core Values		

Essential Habit: Read Your Values Daily to Increase Your Integrity

As you work on reestablishing your identity, it's important to maintain a clear vision of who you hope to become. To accomplish this, make a habit of reminding yourself of your values every day so that you can stay focused on the vision you're trying to create for yourself.

When I did this exercise myself a couple years ago, I wrote all my values down and read them *every single morning*. This helped prime me to consistently behave according to my values – and the habit kept me on track to become the person that I wanted to be.

Chapter 6
Overcoming Low Self-Esteem

"I was always looking outside myself for
strength and confidence but it comes from
within. It is there all the time."

–Anna Freud

After all that talk about identity after stroke, you may feel like something was missing – and your instinct was right. While the 'abilities and desires' concept is central to your sense of identity, it may not be enough to heal your self-image. There's another unexplored factor that plays a large role: self-esteem.

Rebuilding self-esteem after stroke is *essential*, not just for your sense of identity, but for the sake of your recovery too. Low self-esteem can cause you to avoid the challenges and opportunities necessary for a thriving recovery.

High self-esteem helps you persevere when faced with challenge and gives you the motivation to seek out new opportunities for growth. As a result, individuals with high self-esteem will go much farther in their recovery – and in life.

In this chapter, we will discuss the top 3 causes of low self-esteem during stroke recovery and then introduce a great tool to help turn things around. By the end, you'll know how to become a confident person *now* instead of waiting until after your recovery.

Cause #1:
Mistaking Competence for Confidence

There is a common belief that '*competence breeds confidence.*' Meaning, the better you get at something, the more confident you feel. While there is truth behind this saying, it's probably not the best approach during stroke recovery. Competence will come, but it takes a lot of hard work to get there. If you don't have confidence in your potential *first,* it can be very easy to lose hope.

In other words, for stroke recovery, *confidence breeds competence.* Not the other way around.

This is where the paradigm shift happens. If you choose to make this mental switch, self-esteem will have nothing to do with your abilities. Instead, self-esteem will have everything to do with your *beliefs about yourself,* which we will address after covering the next two causes.

Cause #2:
The Wrong Pegs

The second factor that can keep self-esteem low is our 'pegs.' Often, we hang our self-esteem on certain pegs, like physical attractiveness, success, intelligence, strength, etc. And although we feel like these pegs are in our control – they aren't. They never were.

That's where another paradigm shift needs to happen. Although we may have spent our entire life under the illusion that we are in control – an illusion that may have been reinforced by long-term success – we were never *really* in control.

Our success, strength, and appearance (and any other external pegs that we hang our self-esteem on) can all be taken away. And unfortunately, stroke deficits are the best at doing this.

Luckily, this means that we don't need to get back to our 'old self' in order to feel confident again. All we need to do is *choose better pegs* to hang our confidence on – and those better pegs are our *values*.

Our values are a much better source of self-esteem because we have total control over them. Values exist *within* us, not outside of us, and therefore remain constant no matter what obstacle life throws at us.

For example, there was a woman who was one of the first college graduates in her family. Before stroke, she was confident in her new career and loved driving her new expensive car. It was proof of her success.

Then, after a stroke took away her ability to work and drive, her confidence was shattered. All the pegs that she once hung her self-esteem upon were taken away – and she was crushed. However, if she chose to ground her self-esteem in her values, like patience, compassion, and a giving heart, then her confidence would be unshakeable – even after stroke.

With her self-esteem unattached to her external factors and fully attached to her internal compass, she can afford to lose her external sources of confidence and still be okay. She can lose her successes, grace, and status and still be confident because she *trusts herself* to remain patient, compassionate, and generous no matter what.

This example illustrates the shift that needs to happen in order to rebuild self-esteem. We need to shift from external attachments to internal trust. When we learn to shift our source of self-esteem from the things that are missing to the things that are already within us, real confidence emerges.

Do you remember your values that you identified in the previous exercise? They're wonderful sources of self-esteem! And they will always be with you.

Cause #3:
Viewing Yourself as Your Recovery

The third mistake that can keep self-esteem low during stroke recovery is tying our sense of worth to the state of our recovery. When we do this, it gives rise to thoughts like, "I'll feel better in two months when I can move more." Or, "I'll be able to love myself once I can smile like my old self again." And neither of those thoughts help bring lasting confidence. They only delay it.

We don't gain confidence by reducing our disabilities, keeping them hidden, or rushing to reclaim normality, because *confidence cannot be built from shame.* Although shame may feel like a good source of motivation sometimes, it only drives us to try and regain control of our external pegs; which, as we just established, are not a sustainable source of confidence.

To be clear, there is nothing wrong with striving to regain the same life as before. However, if this is causing you to delay your happiness and sense of self-worth, then it's time to identify with something better. By grounding yourself in your highest values, you will build a sustainable source of self-esteem that you can draw upon at any time.

Introducing the 5-Step Framework

Now that we've discussed the top 3 causes of low self-esteem, I'd like to introduce a great tool for understanding how to boost your self-esteem: The 5-Step Framework.

The 5-Step Framework consists of 5 connected steps: Circumstances, Thoughts, Feelings, Actions, and Results. Each step in the Framework leads to the next, always in this order. Our *circumstances* shape our *thoughts*, which then affect our *feelings*, which lead us to take certain *actions* that have specific *results* in our lives.

The dominos do not fall any other way.

By understanding the 5-Step Framework, you can reverse the negative thought patterns that keep self-esteem low. You will see how your thoughts and feelings contribute to your self-esteem and how this directly affects your actions and results.

Understanding the 5-Step Framework

Before we discuss how to apply the 5-Step Framework, let's establish the details first.

Step 1. Circumstances

Circumstances are the *purely factual* happenings of life. For example, "My left arm is paralyzed" is a circumstance. "I will never be able to move my left arm again" is a thought.

Step 2. Thoughts

Your thoughts involve the self-talk that goes on inside your head. Thoughts are biased by our beliefs, both good and bad. Thoughts can be triggered by circumstances, or they can simply come up out of the blue. So, in any given instance, the Framework may start with a circumstance or it may just start with a thought – but it always starts from one of these two places.

Step 3. Feelings

The big difference between thoughts and feelings is that a thought includes a string of words – often whole paragraphs – that occur in your head. A feeling, however, can often be summed up in just one word, and it's felt *in your body*, not just in your head.

Saying "I am angry because she did this to me" is not a feeling – it's a thought. The *feeling* of anger includes a tense, lightheaded, congested vibration in your body, and it can be summed up in just one word: anger.

Our circumstances and thoughts often give rise to specific feelings, which affect us both physically and mentally. For example, angry thoughts can make our blood pressure spike, affect our tone of voice, and give rise to angry emotions. In other words, angry thoughts cause anger (the feeling).

Step 4. Actions

Actions are the steps we take to achieve our goals. Sometimes our actions are obvious and direct, like going to therapy every day. Other times they are indirect, like *not* going to therapy every day. So don't be fooled, inaction is still a type of action.

Whether we take action directly or indirectly, it's important to understand that ALL actions are driven by thoughts and feelings.

If you are feeling excited and motivated, then you will probably take good action. On the flip side, if you are feeling shameful and fearful, you may still take action but it will have a much different result.

Step 5. Results

Results are the consequences of our actions. They are either tangible or intangible. For example, regaining arm movement is a tangible result. Regaining self-esteem is an intangible result. Results are often the thing we crave the most, but they are the last step in the process.

That is why understanding the Framework is the best way to create the results you desire. It will help you figure out which of your thoughts, feelings, and actions may be holding you back, and it will show you where you need to make a change in order to achieve your desired results.

It Always Starts with a Thought

"The mind is everything.
What you think you become."

–Gautama Buddha

Therefore, the best way to create change in any area of your life is by addressing your thoughts first. We cannot control our circumstances, so thoughts are the first step in the Framework that we can control.

Choose your thoughts, choose your results.

And that's where we often make the biggest mistake: we address our thoughts and feelings *last*. We jump ahead in the Framework and attempt to force ourselves to take action to create the results that we want – *assuming* that it will create the feeling we want. But thoughts and feelings always come before actions and results – not after.

For example, let's say that you force yourself to go to the gym and workout every day (action) so that you can lose weight (result) and then feel confident (feeling) about your body.

After looking at the 5-Step Framework, you will realize that this approach is out of order. Action is the *middle* step, and the *feeling of confidence* should come first.

If we don't consider the thoughts and feelings that come before our actions, we're skipping two steps – and this makes it extremely difficult to create change. The 5-Step Framework must be followed *sequentially* if we want to create lasting results.

For example, let's say that a young male stroke survivor is devastated by the losses associated with his stroke, especially at such a young age. He can't play sports with his friends anymore and his self-esteem has taken a huge hit. These days he feels depressed and full of shame.

In an attempt to get back to 'normal,' he forces himself to go to therapy, but his depression weighs on him. He barely has enough willpower to get started and rarely finishes his exercises. He persists through his shame, though, and eventually makes an improvement that gives him a little bit of self-esteem back. However, the journey ahead is long and dreary, and he doesn't feel motivated to continue.

In this example, long-term change will be hard for the young stroke survivor because he put the cart before the horse. He assumed that his actions would create the feeling that he wanted – but that's not how the dominos fall.

The best way of creating change is to *create the thoughts and feelings first*.

Because if we focus on our actions first – fueled by shame and low self-esteem – then our results will be tainted with shame and self-doubt. But if you generate confident thoughts and confident feelings *before* taking action, then you will be operating from a confident place. This will inevitably lead to better results – the kind of results that you can only get through *already* feeling confident.

How to Apply the 5-Step Framework

To create whatever change you want to see in your life – start by addressing your thoughts first.

Try asking yourself, "Once I achieve a recovery that is acceptable to me, what would I believe about myself? What would I think and feel about myself, my present situation, and my future?" Take some time right now to reflect on that question and see what kind of answers come forward.

Now, start thinking those thoughts *now*.

Start generating confident thoughts and confidence will trickle down into your feelings, actions, and results. Because when we *think* confidently, then we *feel* confident, and then we *act* with confidence – and we see the *result* of becoming confident.

That's how the 5-Step Framework works.

Using the Framework to Boost Self-Esteem

A survivor once told me that she felt like she couldn't feel good about herself until she could walk normally again. She felt embarrassed when she was out in public because she felt like others would stare at her and judge her disability. She felt like she would only be able to feel good again once her deficits were no longer visible.

After hearing this, I asked her what thoughts were creating those feelings of low self-esteem, and she responded, "I think people assume I'm dumb. I think they see what's wrong on the outside, and assume something's wrong on the inside, too."

So I asked her to change that thought and assume that the opposite is true. Whenever she felt judged by others, I asked her to start thinking, "They must assume I'm very strong to be walking with my disability in the first place."

This puts her in a much more compassionate, empowering place. And if she continues to *assume the best in others and herself*, then those compassionate thoughts will trickle down into all her feelings, actions, and results. That's the best way to boost self-esteem.

So if feeling judged by others is keeping your self-esteem low, then you may be guilty of assuming the worst in others, too. You may assume that others are thinking rude thoughts – but no one can ever *really* know what's going on in someone else's head. All we can do is make assumptions.

So a much better alternative to assuming the worst in others is to try and assume the best! Those thoughts will create the *feeling* of self-compassion, which is a sweet, tender feeling that will motivate the best actions and create the best results because you will be operating from the heart.

This is where true healing and happiness comes from. By mastering the ability to generate positive thoughts, all of your feelings, actions, and results will be fueled by love.

And love can move mountains.

Time and Practice

As with all skills, it takes time and practice to develop healthy self-esteem. Often, there are persistent negative thoughts keeping us stuck in self-conscious feelings. And in order to reverse that habit, we have to intentionally choose positive thoughts over and over and over again.

So be patient with yourself. Personal change does not happen overnight. It happens over the course of months and years of steady effort.

To help keep you on track, the following Exercise and Essential Habit will help you apply the Framework to rebuild your self-esteem. I encourage you to try them for at least a month and see how it goes. Remember, confidence is built over time, not all at once.

Exercise: Applying the Framework to Boost Self-Esteem

During this exercise, we are going to apply the 5-Step Framework to reverse negative thoughts and feelings by re-placing them with positive ones. Here we will be dealing specifically with low self-esteem, but you can use this exercise for reversing any and all negative thoughts and feelings.

So first, think of a time where you were feeling particularly low and felt like your self-esteem was shot. Then, copy the chart on the following page in your stroke recovery journal and go through all 5 steps.

Event	Thought	Feeling	Action	Result
This is the circumstance	What did you think?	How did you feel?	What did the feeling cause you to do or not do?	What was the outcome of your action or inaction?
Not every Framework will start with an event, but most will	What thoughts did the event trigger?	Boil it down into one word		
Here, simply write down what happened	Or, what thoughts came out of the blue?			
Use purely facts				

For the event, write down exactly what happened. Use strictly facts. Avoid using descriptive language as it usually implies an opinion.

For the thought, write down all the thoughts you had. They don't have to be the exact ones, but try to remember what you were thinking as best you can.

For the feeling, boil everything down into one word – and one word only – to describe how you felt.

For the action, write down what these thoughts and feelings caused you to do.

And for the result, write down the outcome of your action.

To illustrate this process, let's say that I slipped on a banana peel at the mall in front of a bunch of people. The Framework on the following page provides an example of how the chart can be filled out.

Event	Thought	Feeling	Action	Result
I slipped on a banana peel	That hurt but at least I'm okay	Proud	Picked myself up and continued on my way	Got those new jeans I wanted
	I'm sure everyone is staring because they're wondering if I'm okay too			
	I'm proud for getting back up each time I fall			

Once you've completed the chart, draw another one and write down the same event as before. Then in the thought section, replace the old, negative thoughts from your first chart with something far more positive. Once you've done that, go through the next 3 steps and write down what *would* have happened with the new thought.

The Framework on the following page is an example of how the previous chart can be rewritten.

Event	Thought	Feeling	Action	Result
I slipped on a banana peel	I'm so clumsy I always do this My balance is so bad Why does everyone have to stare Its' so rude When will I stop doing things like this?	Embarrassed	Left the mall immediately	Did not get to buy the new jeans I wanted

After you do this exercise yourself, you will see how a simple shift in your thoughts can create a world of difference in your results!

Essential Habit: Generate Confident Thoughts Daily to Increase Self-Esteem

Take the previous exercise, and perform it on the idea of your most confident self. Think about the thoughts and feelings that would go into creating that confidence, and fill out the chart in your stroke recovery journal.

Then, make a habit of looking at it every morning so that you know exactly where to focus your thoughts throughout the day. Remembering to choose confident thoughts is the best way to boost self-esteem.

Chapter 7
Motivating Your Mindset

"Strength does not come from what you can do. It comes from overcoming the things you once thought you couldn't."

–Rikki Rogers

Up until now, you've been mastering your mindset. You've been learning, reflecting, and digging deep down into your psyche to discover your inner workings and master your thought patterns. And now you're ready to take action, which is often the most difficult part.

Typically, when we face serious challenges, we avoid action like the plague. We find ways to procrastinate, delay, and neglect the things that need doing. But *doing* is the only way to see results.

Since this whole book is laced with action, I won't overwhelm you with (too many) more things to do. Instead, this chapter will provide some actionable advice that can help you stay motivated to take the action you need to achieve an amazing recovery.

The Price of Forgetting

"When thou art troubled about anything,
thou hast forgotten."

–Marcus Aurelius

I'd like to start with a short lesson from my favorite Stoic philosopher: Marcus Aurelius.

Marcus Aurelius was a Roman emperor who kept a personal diary about his stoic philosophies and ethics. Marcus didn't write these letters hoping that one day they'd become famous and published (although, that's exactly what happened with the book *Meditations*). Instead, Marcus wrote those letters to help himself *remember*.

He understood that unless he was reminded of his strong ethics, he would easily forget them. So he continuously wrote and reflected on his entries to remind himself of the lessons he learned. Otherwise, he knew that history would repeat itself.

Marcus realized that simple reminders are the best way to stay motivated on the path towards self-improvement. And he practiced what he preached (or rather, wrote), earning himself the title as one of the Five Good Emperors. With such a prestigious reputation, I hope we can feel confident in the importance of this whole *remembering* thing.

Because when we forget, we make the same mistakes over and over again.

We forget about our goals and the vision that we're trying to create for ourselves. We forget that we need to remain aware of our emotions and reactions. We forget that we promised ourselves we'd exercise. We forget that our intention was to stick this out until the end.

Sometimes, we simply forget.

And that's why remembering is critical during stroke recovery. Because when you remember your mistakes, you get to avoid repeating them. When you remember your victories, you get to relish in gratitude. And when you remember how far you've come, you find the motivation to keep taking action.

This is why your stroke recovery journal is so essential on your road to recovery. It helps you keep track of all the insights that you uncover, so that you can reflect back on them and remember – just like Marcus.

Now that you know why remembrance is crucial, we're going to dive right into the good stuff on motivation and taking action – starting with a growth mindset.

Developing a Growth Mindset

A growth mindset is key for achieving success. In order to appreciate the importance of a growth mindset, let's first discuss its opposite: a fixed mindset.

Those with a fixed mindset hold on tight to their limiting beliefs. They resist the idea that their situation can change and partially or fully believe that their disabilities are set in stone. This discourages them from taking action because they don't think results will come. In other words, action is only seen as a waste of effort.

Someone with a growth mindset, however, may have limiting beliefs, but they're willing to reconsider them and replace them with better ones. (You're reading a self-help book, so that's probably you!)

Growth-minded individuals see their potential, which encourages them to take action in order to see the results that they want. And even if they fail, they learn from it and know it's only a matter of time until they succeed.

So, the next time you feel stuck somewhere in your recovery, try to identify exactly where you feel a sense of permanence. Then, gently tell yourself, like you would a friend, that your situation is not permanent. It *is* changeable – and you have the power to make that change.

Identify the challenge and *lean into it*. And even if you fail, you're already moving in the right direction.

For example, when you feel like you've hit a plateau, it can make you feel stuck in your recovery. Suddenly, your limitations feel permanent, and it's a dreadful feeling that can spiral into a fixed mindset.

To avoid this slip, you can turn inward and identify where you feel stuck. Then, instead of assuming permanence, you can identify the available opportunity or challenge, and then lean into it. This will help you create a growth mindset around your situation. As a result, you may realize that you're not stuck after all, and that challenge and practice can help.

Positive and Negative Motivators

Another great motivation tactic includes identifying your motivation type. This will help you systematically focus your efforts and exploit your strengths, which will speed everything along.

As a brief overview, there are three types of motivators: positive, negative, and identity motivators. Identity motivators deserve a section of their own, so we'll talk about the other two types first.

Positive motivators inspire us to gain something good, whereas negative motivators push us to avoid something bad. Although it sounds like these two types of motivators could inspire the same amount of action, that's not always the case.

With negative motivators, your actions are caused by the desire to *avoid pain*. During stroke recovery, this can manifest as the motivation to get past recovery because it's painful and uncomfortable; and that pain and discomfort can serve as effective short-term motivation.

In the long-term, however, your motivation will diminish after you achieve some success because your pain has diminished. The fire that you needed to keep yourself going is slowly being put out. And while it's certainly a good fire to put out (since that fire was causing pain), you will eventually stop seeing the point of continuing your efforts.

For example, let's say you feel embarrassed because you have difficulty balancing, which causes you to trip and stumble while out in public. As a result, these negative feelings motivate you to work really hard at regaining your balance during therapy. And then, after months of effort, you successfully regain some of your balance and no longer stumble while out in public. You feel great!

But now that the pain is gone, you start procrastinating with your other exercises. You are not as motivated because you're not as embarrassed anymore. While it's fantastic that you are no longer embarrassed, you may find that your recovery begins to flat line because the fire to push through has diminished. Now, you're stuck.

As you can see, the link between pain and motivation can be dangerous for someone who uses negative motivators. While it can serve as effective motivation in the beginning, it's best to transition to other types of motivation if you want to keep making progress.

This is where positive motivators shine! With a positive motivator, you're inspired by what you could achieve in the future instead of what you hate about the present. This offers much better long-term drive for your stroke recovery efforts. If negative motivators are the spark, positive motivators are the fuel.

By focusing on your limitless potential, your motivation will increase as your results increase. Each time you level up, there will be another sweet reward waiting for you, and everything keeps getting better and better. And with this momentum, you will produce far better results.

Let's take a different look at our previous example. Let's say that you don't really care about what anyone thinks of you. You just want to regain balance for your own satisfaction, and ultimately you want to achieve a full recovery.

As you persist in your recovery and regain more balance, you become excited. Your efforts are producing results, and now you want *more*. Instead of slowing down as you achieve success, you speed up. You continue to exercise consistently (without burning yourself out, of course), and in a few years' time, you achieve the recovery you desire!

Positive motivators can produce far better results because they make you *excited* instead of appeased. You enter an upward spiral of success that can't be matched by negative motivation.

As the saying goes, "Energy flows where attention goes." And if your attention is focused on what you have to gain instead of what you can't afford to lose, everything changes.

Identity-Based Motivation

*"You cannot perform in a manner
inconsistent with the way you see yourself."*

–Zig Ziglar

Identity-based motivation, the third type of motivator, occurs when you choose to identify yourself with motivating characteristics, like discipline and hard work. This way, instead of working towards something good or away from something bad, you persist because *it's part of who you are.*

This concept is related to the ideas covered in Chapter 5 and the importance of your *values* and the role they play in your sense of self. But this time we're going to apply the principle in reverse.

Instead of scaling your desires *back* to suit your values, you can also scale you values *forward* to suit your future desires. Meaning, try to identify yourself with motivating characteristics *even if you don't possess those qualities yet.* Because once you make the choice to identify with them, they will influence your thoughts, which – as you know from the Framework – will have a ripple effect into your actions and motivation.

For example, let's say that you somehow managed to coast along your entire life (most likely with plenty of talent and also plenty of luck) and you began to identify yourself as someone who achieved a lot of success with little effort. Because you've identified yourself in this way, it will be difficult for you to enjoy working hard because it's 'just not who you are.'

And that's where we make the switch. By choosing to make ambition and determination – or any other motivating characteristic that will advance your recovery – a part of who you are, you can automatically increase your motivation to act that way.

So, what qualities do you wish you had? What qualities do all successful survivors have in common? What would move your recovery along the fastest?

Once you answer these questions, start pretending like you already own those qualities. Generate the thoughts and feelings now, and eventually it will stick. As a result, those awesome qualities will just become *you*.

Positive Illusion

Our second-to-last motivation tactic is positive illusion, which is the art of purposeful self-delusion. Most of the time self-delusion is seen as a bad thing, but *purposeful* self-delusion can be incredibly beneficial.

Earlier in this book, I told you that you should believe in a full recovery. I said that even if you can't achieve a full recovery, simply believing that you can will get you much farther than believing you can't. This is an example of a positive illusion.

Our thoughts create our reality, and if we think we can't do something, we won't. Sometimes we won't even attempt to.

And I'd much rather have you attempt to do something and fail than not attempt it at all. Success is only achieved through action, and it doesn't matter whether that action feels purposeful or like a shot in the dark. All that matters is that you tried. And that's what positive illusions are good for – fueling your motivation to give it your best shot.

So go ahead, believe in something crazy! Believe in a full recovery. Believe in using both hands to cook again. Believe in something that no one else thinks is possible, because I bet that you can prove them wrong.

I *know* that you can prove them wrong.

Better Goals

The final motivational tactic is called *outcome-oriented goal-setting*. Sound boring? Hopefully not the way I'm serving it.

Sometimes 'normal' goals fail to motivate you because they lack meaning and vision. In other words, they don't tell you *why* you should take action. Instead, they only tell you *what* to do and by when. But the *why* is what matters most – and that's exactly what outcome-oriented goal-setting is all about.

Unlike normal goals, outcome-oriented goals clearly illustrate the benefits and losses associated with action and inaction. Each goal states exactly what you should do, *why* you should do it, and *what you could gain* from taking that action or *what you could lose* from inaction (i.e. the outcomes).

When you paint the picture this way, it makes the benefits much more tangible. And when you can see the benefits clearly, you are inspired to take far more action. If you find yourself thinking, "Hmmm. Maybe this outcome-oriented goal thing is worth a shot," then I recommend trying the following exercise.

Exercise: Setting Outcome-Oriented Goals

Copy the following chart in your stroke recovery journal and identify three goals that you want to achieve in your recovery. These could be things you're already working towards or ones you have been putting off. Then, for each of these goals, write down the following:

- All the pain associated with reaching the goal (the current barriers between you and your goal)

- The benefits of procrastination (what you gain from not taking action)

- The cost of not taking the action (what you lose from not taking action)

- The benefits of taking action (what you gain from taking action)

Try and think in terms of your health, self-esteem, relationships, and independence. Write down as much as you can.

After you complete this exercise, watch what it does to your motivation. Previously, you may not have realized what you were losing from not taking action, and this exercise helps paint a clear picture. Or, perhaps you didn't realize exactly what you have to gain, and now you're even more excited about taking action.

Goal	Pain	Gain	Cost	Benefit
What do you hope to achieve?	What is the pain associated with achieving that goal?	What are the benefits of procrastination? What do you gain by not taking action?	What is the cost of procrastination? What do you lose by procrastinating?	What would you gain by achieving your goals?

Essential Habit: Read Your Goals Daily to Increase Your Motivation

Once you establish your goals, don't let the motivation to reach them leave you. In other words, don't let yourself forget! Instead, bookmark the page you just wrote in your stroke recovery journal and make a habit of reading it *every single morning* – along with your values. A simple reminder like this can reap big benefits on your road to recovery.

There may be a part of you that says, "How could I possibly forget about overcoming the thing that turned my life upside-down?" But try not to dismiss this idea. Even the most motivated individuals in the world have a system to keep themselves on track.

Reminders are not a sign of weakness.

They're a form of strength.

Chapter 8
Becoming Fearless

"Sometimes the smallest step in the right direction ends up being the biggest step of your life. Tip toe if you must, but take the step."

–Naeem Callaway

As you start taking action towards your recovery, you may find yourself face-to-face with one of the greatest obstacles of all: fear. This sneaky feeling often disguises itself as other negative emotions like anxiety, depression, and even procrastination – but it always plays the same game: keeping you away from your dreams and the recovery you deserve.

When we feel fear and anxiety, we often like to take massive action in order to remove ourselves from the situation. This massive action can either burn us out or – if it's massive inaction – keep us stuck.

Although it can be particularly tough to deal with fear, there is a scientifically proven process for overcoming it. This chapter will explain that process and show you how visualization can help.

First, let's take a look at the origin of fear.

Our Fight-or-Flight Response

Fear is triggered by our fight-or-flight response, which is a physiological reaction to something threatening. The response comes from our primal instinct to protect ourselves from danger, and it's vital for our survival. For example, back in the days of hunting and gathering, our fight-or-flight response gave us the adrenaline we needed to run from a wild animal.

These days, however, our flight-or-flight response can be triggered by much smaller events, like doing rehabilitation exercises. Even though rehabilitation places you in no real harm, just the thought of exercising can still trigger fear. As a result, this fear can prevent you from taking action, which leads to a vicious downward, unproductive spiral.

Luckily, we can take specific steps to stop this mechanism from being triggered. The first step involves 'turning off' your amygdala.

Your Well-Meaning Amygdala

The amygdala is an almond-shaped part of our brain involved with emotion regulation. Of particular interest, the amygdala is where the *fight-or-flight response* starts in our bodies.

The purpose of your amygdala is to prepare you for combat (fight) or escape (flight) by revving your body up with energizing hormones. This maximizes your alertness and responsivity to the environment so that you can respond as best you can.

Your amygdala has good intentions. After all, our ancestors would have been eaten by bears if it weren't for the amygdala's help. However, sometimes our amygdala can be a little *too* sensitive. During stroke recovery, for example, feelings of job insecurity and shame can cause your amygdala to release energizing hormones, which, without a real threat to spend that energy on, often leads to anxiety.

Then, in our attempt to ease this anxiety, we often try to take *massive action* in order to quickly remove ourselves from the threatening situation. For example, we decide to work our butts off during therapy in order to save ourselves from the looming threat of job termination and embarrassment.

Unfortunately, such massive action often leads to burnout, and – what's worse – further stimulates our amygdala, which amplifies our fight-or-flight response even more. As a result, we grow even *more* anxious and the vicious cycle continues.

To end the fearful cycle, try to realize that stroke recovery is not what's causing your fear – the well-meaning biological reaction from your amygdala is. And you can turn your amygdala off by asking yourself small questions.

Turning Fear Off

When we ask our subconscious mind questions, it will always give us an answer. Unfortunately, when we worry, we tend to ask ourselves worst-case scenario questions like, "What will happen if I fail? What if I can't get through this? How long is this whole thing going to take?"

And when you ask yourself extreme questions, your mind will logically answer with extreme answers! And that's guaranteed to trigger fear.

To turn this around, try asking yourself smaller questions that lean towards optimism instead of worry. By asking yourself positive questions, your mind will respond with positive answers! It really is that simple.

For example, try to avoid asking yourself big, negative questions like, "What will happen if no one can look after me? What would happen if I never get better?"

Instead, try asking yourself smaller, optimistic questions like, "Who can I contact today that might be able to help me out later? What small action can I take today that will get me one inch closer to my recovery goals?"

This keeps you focused on taking positive action instead of slipping into the grips of anxiety and procrastination. And best of all, your amygdala stays out of the picture.

Small Actions, Big Results

"No matter what, you can always fight the battles of just today. It's only when you add the infinite battles of yesterday and tomorrow that life gets overly complicated."

-Marc Chernoff

Asking yourself *small questions* isn't the only way to turn off fear. As I mentioned above, trying to take massive action only revs up your amygdala. So instead, you should try and break your goals down into manageable chunks. In other words, take *small actions*, too.

Although it seems like taking small actions would slow everything down, it can actually speed the recovery process along because it keeps you hammering away bit by bit, instead of procrastinating about taking that one giant leap.

Now, don't get me wrong. Giant leaps are good, especially when they're leaps of faith. But when our primary source of motivation for taking that leap is fear, it can lead to catastrophe when we fall.

Instead, the key is to *scale back* and reduce the size of the step you're taking when you feel afraid. This makes action much more doable and far less stressful, which keeps fear out of the picture.

For example, focusing on the long road to recovery ahead of you can easily make you overwhelmed. All the problems and tasks that need attention come pouring down on you all at once. It's not just scary, it's paralyzing! A much better approach is taking your recovery day-by-day.

This does not mean you should forgo planning and goal-setting. You should absolutely have a long-term plan and outcome-oriented goals written down somewhere you look frequently. However, once you have a goal, you should keep your focus only on what you have to do *today* – not this week/month/year – in order to accomplish it.

By narrowing your focus to what you need to accomplish today, instead of the infinite tasks of the future, you can keep fear at bay. Taking action becomes much easier when you focus on the inch right in front of you instead of the miles ahead.

Excitement – The Fearless Emotion

Now, some of you may be thinking, "What about Bill Gates? What about Steve Jobs? What about all the successful people who take really big steps and accomplish really big things? It doesn't look like fear is getting in their way. Why are they so different from me?"

Ah yes, those people.

Those people harness a secret weapon. Although it seems like they achieve incredible success through massive action and hard work, what you fail to see is what's going on *underneath*. And I'm willing to bet that the driving force underneath all that massive action is a big pool of *excitement* – because excitement is another way to turn fear off.

Something about excitement works well with our brain, shutting down our amygdala and keeping our fight-or-flight response off. When facing an obstacle that you feel ill-equipped to handle, you can instantly become motivated to start working by simply getting downright *excited*.

Have you ever felt so excited about an idea that you couldn't wait to start working on it? Perhaps it was a creative project or a new hobby. Whatever it was, do you remember feeling that thing bubbling up in your chest trying to make its way into this world?

Try to recreate that feeling about your recovery, as silly and impossible as it may sound. At first you may only find the energy to get excited about the end goal, and that's great! From there, try to work your way up to getting excited about the *process*, too.

If you can manage to get excited about both the end goal and everything in between, then procrastination and fear won't stand a chance.

Mental Magic

Now you have the full recipe for managing fear: asking small questions, taking small steps, and getting *downright excited* about it! Simple enough. Now we're going to take the whole process to the next level by incorporating the most useful exercise into your recovery – *mental practice*.

Mental practice, or *visualization*, is the art of imagining yourself doing something in your head. This tactic can help squash fear, motivate effective action, and *boost mobility*. It might sound crazy, but it works because you have neuroplasticity on your side.

Each time you mentally practice something, you trigger neuroplasticity the same way that physical practice does.[2] Plus, while you're rewiring your mind to be able to accomplish an action, you're also getting nice and comfortable with the idea of taking that action – which, again, helps squash fear.

There are many studies proving the efficacy for mental practice for stroke recovery, but they've all been conducted within the last couple decades (starting in the early 2000's).[3] However, the phenomenon has been used for eons by musicians and athletes to improve their performance.

One notable example is Michael Phelps. This 23-time gold medal winner (at the time of writing) used mental practice to give him an edge in his sport. By rewiring his mind through rigorous physical *and* mental practice, he did everything he could to prepare himself for the Olympics. And with 23 gold medals under his belt, we can all agree that it works.

The same concept applies directly to stroke recovery. For example, if you don't have the ability to walk independently yet, then try spending time every morning visualizing yourself walking. Each time you repeat this mental practice, the connections in your brain responsible for walking become stronger and stronger, just like physical practice. Then, in due time, you will see improvements in your actual walking ability.

When impairments are severe, the results will come slowly – almost painstakingly so – but when you're trying to achieve a specific goal, any sign of progress is reason to keep going! And once you regain enough movement to start physical practice, you can start adding physical exercise to your regimen as well.

Please note that although it may be tempting to forgo your visualization practices once you start to see results, try to stick with it. It's important to keep the habit up because combining physical and mental practice together has been proven to produce even better results.[4]

So, if you're ready to start implementing this game-changing practice, use the following two visualization exercises to get started.

Exercise: Self-Guided Visualizations

If you're just starting visualization for the first time, start simple. Pick one activity or movement that you'd like to do better and visualize yourself doing that one thing. Practice this visualization every day. While you're imagining it, I recommend either laying down or sitting upright with your eyes closed.

Begin each visualization session with 10-20 deep breaths to clear your mind. Take your time with this. Then, move into the visualization and include *as many sensory details as you can.*

What will it sound like? What will it feel like? What will it look, taste, and smell like?

The more descriptive you are in your visualizations, the more of your brain you will engage, and the more powerful your results will be. So allow yourself this time to be creative.

Try visualizing yourself in unique places, like at the beach with the sand in between your toes and a cool ocean breeze brushing against your face. The more compelling the imagery, the more your neuroplasticity will be engaged.

Then, try to spend at least five minutes each day performing this visualization. And if you want to go deeper into your practice, try adding the following exercise.

Exercise: Audio-Based Guided Visualization

For this immersive form of mental practice, you will need to create an audio recording that will guide you through your visualization practice.

In your recording, include a full description of the task you want to perform in overwhelming sensory detail. Describe all the sights, sounds, smells, and even tastes of what you're doing. Continue to describe everything about the situation for as long as you can (ideally 3-5 minutes).

Here's an example for walking:

"Imagine that you're standing in your doorway. Feel the sturdy hardwood floor beneath your feet. You're standing tall, and the room feels warm and comfortable. Now imagine that you take your first step forward as you plant your right foot firmly on the hardwood floor. As you take your next step, your body begins to move fluidly across the room..."

And later the details are filled in:

"Feel yourself take each step with intention and grace, and feel the weight of your body roll through your heels and into your toes as you push off the ground. Feel your knees bend and straighten as you continue to take one step after another..."

Once you complete your audio recording, listen to it every day. When you feel ready, try some physical practice to see if you've improved. As much as possible, continue to use mental and physical practice together.

Essential Habit: Visualize Your Goals for One Minute a Day to Increase Your Success

When beginning a visualization practice, it's easy to start off gung-ho by spending twenty minutes each day visualizing your goal. However, if you don't see immediate results, it will rapidly diminish your motivation to keep up the habit. To avoid this burnout, be sure to take small steps.

Start by spending one quick minute every morning visualizing your goal. One minute – that's all you need in the beginning. It may not sound effective, but it's long enough to initiate changes in the brain and short enough to help make it a habit.

Then, once you've gone two weeks straight with your one minute visualizations, slowly start to increase your time. Perhaps you try two minutes, or five. It doesn't matter. Go at your own pace, and continue to slowly increase your sessions until you've developed a deep and sustainable practice.

Chapter 9
Creating Your Happy Brain

"The happiness of your life depends upon
the quality of your thoughts"

−Marcus Aurelius

We can all agree that becoming fearless helps make stroke recovery easier. Now imagine what could happen if you worked on becoming happier, too.

This chapter will focus on how brain mechanics play a role in happiness. There won't be any explicit advice like "do this one thing and you'll be happy," because advice like that doesn't work. Telling yourself to "just be happy" won't work either because there are so many factors that impact your happiness.

That's why this chapter is called "Creating Your Happy Brain" instead of "How to Be Happy." We're going to focus on managing your thoughts – because that's where every emotion starts.

Positive Neuroplasticity

"Neurons that fire together, wire together."

–Donald Hebb

I've been talking about neuroplasticity throughout this entire book, and I've mentioned in bits and pieces how neuroplasticity can rewire your brain for a positive mindset. Now I'd like to dig much deeper into this concept.

There's a phenomenon called *experience-dependent neuroplasticity*, which refers to how the brain changes during our daily experiences. This means that whatever you repeatedly experience and think about becomes part of your neural structure. In other words, whatever you repeatedly rest your mind on becomes part of your brain.

Through this discovery, science has shown that you need to be extremely careful about where you focus your attention. For example, if you want to create a life of happiness, you shouldn't allow your mind to consistently think about worst-case scenarios. This will only reinforce the neural connections responsible for negative thinking!

Luckily the opposite is also true. If you repeatedly focus on the best-case scenarios, you will naturally become a more optimistic and resilient person. This is why banishing limiting beliefs and focusing on a full recovery is so important. Because when you repeatedly focus your attention on your potential, you help make it a reality.

As you can see, experience-dependent neuroplasticity can be great news for everybody who knows how to harness it, and it's especially great during stroke recovery. Experience-dependent neuroplasticity means that unwanted feelings of frustration, anger, and fear can be rewired through repetitive practice for a sustained length of time.

But before we discuss how to accomplish that, let's discuss why you may have these negative feelings in the first place.

The Negativity Bias

From the Framework in Chapter 6, we know that feelings come from our thoughts. So if we want to generate the feeling of happiness, we have to start by generating happy thoughts. However, this can be very difficult if our *negativity bias* is too strong.

Our negativity bias is the natural tendency for negative things to stick in our minds like glue. It's why we remember that one irritating thing our doctor said, yet we forget about the dozens of small favors our nurses have done for us. Our negativity bias trains our brain to remember bad moments, but not good ones.

You may wonder why we would have such an awful mechanism ingrained in our brain – but it's there for good reason. Our negativity bias keeps us safe from danger by heightening our response to negative stimuli. For example, we don't touch open flames because we remember that they cause pain, even if we only experience that pain once in our lives. Unfortunately, if we allow our negativity bias to become too strong, it can dominate our lives.

There are two reasons why this can happen. First, when we experience something good, it's often perceived as *finished* instead of a continuous experience. And when we're finished with something, our mind quickly moves on to the next thing instead of relishing in the good feeling.

As an example, let's say you got farther along in your hand exercises today than you did yesterday. That's a great accomplishment! But instead of taking time to relish in the feeling of accomplishment or write it down in your journal, the natural tendency is to quickly move on to the next problem waiting to be solved.

This doesn't help create a happy brain.

Your Brain's Default Mode

The second biological hindrance to happiness is your brain's Default Mode Network. Although the following description of this network may sound similar to your negativity bias, it's a completely separate mechanism.

Your Default Mode Network is a system of interacting brain regions that are responsible for problem solving when your mind is on autopilot. It's the 'default software' in your brain that causes you to subconsciously scan your life for problems when you're not paying attention to your thoughts. As you can imagine, this can easily lead to discontent if left unchecked.

Your Default Mode Network has been shaping your neural structure for your entire life because these thoughts, whether we notice them or not, become habits. For instance, the more you allow your brain to wander into problem-solving mode, the more skillful you will become at finding problems in your daily life – even if those problems don't really exist!

Conversely, the more you focus on positive things, the more skillful you will become at finding moments of joy in your daily life. And that's exactly what we're going to do.

Becoming Positive by Default

To use neuroplasticity to boost your happiness, we're going to create a *positivity bias* for our brains to replace our old software. We will achieve this by becoming aware of our wandering mind and relentlessly trying to live in the present moment. In other words, we will embrace *mindfulness*, which is what the next chapter will cover in more detail.

As a starting point, it's a good idea to try and gauge how often your mind wanders. You will find an exercise for this at the end of the chapter, so if you want more details on what to do, feel free to jump ahead to that section.

To put it briefly, you will pick a five-hour period during your day and set a timer to go off every 15 minutes. Then, every time the timer goes off, pause what you are doing and notice what you're thinking about at that time. This will give you an idea of how often your mind wanders and what it tends to focus on when it does.

As fair warning, when researchers conducted an experiment very similar to this, they found that almost half our thoughts are completely unrelated to what we're actually doing.[5] And what's worse, they found that most of our wandering thoughts do a poor job of promoting our own happiness. The good news is that once we recognize this, we can actively work to correct the problem and increase our happiness.

There are two steps involved with this. First, you need to become aware of *when* your mind wanders. Then you need to learn how to pull your mind back into the present moment when it does wander. Or, if the present moment isn't exactly a source of joy, you can redirect your wandering mind to think about previous positive experiences.

Let's start by digging further into the first step.

The Power of Presence

When you live in the present moment, the problems of the past and future fade and you're left with what's here – which is always more manageable than the endless problems of the past and anticipated problems of the future.

The simple act of focusing on the present moment is a huge step towards creating your happy brain because it shuts your problem-solving Default Mode Network *off*. By focusing on the present moment, you get better at *staying* in the present. And when you do this repeatedly, a more peaceful you will start to emerge.

For example, if you go on a walk around your neighborhood, try to focus only on the walk. Feel the concrete beneath your feet, the fresh air in your lungs, and the way your body moves. Even if some of your body's movements are uncomfortable, it's much better to feel the discomfort and stay with yourself than to allow your mind to leave you.

Some of you may be thinking, "But I enjoy day dreaming when I go for walks. What's wrong with that?" And there's nothing wrong with that! If your mind wanders onto positive thoughts and you don't have a problem with it – then keep at it! Each time you focus on the positive, you're creating a more positive neural structure. You are building a happy brain!

However, if you find that your mind tends to wander onto negative thoughts, then simply being aware of those thoughts might not be enough. You will also have to learn how to change your wandering thoughts to be more positive. Fortunately, this is possible by using the following method.

The Positivity Bias

If you want to rewire your mind for happiness, you need to learn to override your natural negativity bias with a *positivity bias*. To do this, you have to make positive experiences stick to your mind like glue. In time, these positive experiences will then 'crowd out' the bad. This requires serious effort, awareness, and time; but it's worth it for the sake of creating a positive mindset.

In order to develop a positivity bias, you need to really soak in all of your positive experiences. Remember, the brain naturally doesn't hang onto these experiences as strongly as it does with negative experiences. Therefore, in order to create a positivity bias, you have to pay close attention to your thoughts.

For starters, remember to cherish all of your positive experiences throughout the day. Each time something good happens, allow yourself to linger. Relish the moment and let the good soak in. This will let the positive experience create positive changes in the brain.

This is a very rewarding practice because stroke recovery is *full* of things to celebrate; and we might miss it unless we start paying careful attention to our automatic thoughts.

The more you take in the positive, the better you will become at finding things to feel good about. With enough practice, your brain will naturally seek out things to feel good about even without your conscious effort. In other words, being positive will become effortless.

If this feels out of reach for you, I promise that it's not. Creating a positivity bias just requires a consistent, dedicated practice of noticing the good.

Feelings Are for Feeling

"Whatever comes, let it come,
what stays let stay,
what goes let go."

−Papaji

Now, after reading this chapter, it may feel like I'm glossing over the very challenging hardships involved with stroke recovery. So I'd like to end on an important note:

Your job is not to be happy all the time.

Your job is to allow yourself to *feel all your feelings, even the bad ones.*

That way, when negative emotions do arise – which they always will, no matter how well your brain becomes wired for happiness – you will have the strength to *let them in*, to let them wash over you, and then release them. Because we cannot release something we resist. Resistance only makes a negative emotion stronger. We have to first own and fully embrace the emotion before it can leave.

By feeling *all* your feelings instead of resisting the ones you don't want, there won't be any part of yourself that you can't face. With this mindset, you'll be able to handle every emotion that comes your way by simply *allowing yourself to feel them*.

And it will empower you.

You won't keel over when negativity inevitably strikes. You'll be able to stay grounded in your truth and honor whatever feeling is there. As a result, you'll find a much greater capacity to enjoy those happy moments when they inevitably come around, too.

Because the reality is that some days will be happier than others. And the goal is to welcome happiness when it comes and avoid getting frustrated when positive thinking doesn't work. Otherwise you may fall into a dangerous feedback loop, which can look like the following example.

Let's say that you're having a bad day, and at this point you've developed enough self-awareness to identify the thoughts that are creating your despair. But no matter how hard you try, you can't shake it.

You try to reverse the negative belief and recite positive sentences over and over, but you still can't escape the feeling. Now you're frustrated. It feels like the concepts you learned in this chapter suck. Then this frustration becomes a second layer on top of your despair. The feedback loop continues, and it can quickly spiral out of control.

This is why it's important to honor *all* of your feelings – the good and the bad. Because you're human and you will experience both. And it's impossible to generate positive thoughts all the time.

So when you're feeling down, allow yourself to experience the truth of that feeling. Be sure to exercise as much self-compassion as you can. By allowing yourself to feel all your experiences, not just the positive ones, you become *authentic*. You start to honor your truth – the full story of who you are – and that's a great place to be.

Then, when you're feeling happy, soak it up! Relish in the feeling and be grateful. Allow the experience to create positive changes in your brain.

Remember, you are the commander of this ship. And while you can't control the weather, you can control how you steer the vessel.

Exercise: Discover Your Default Mode Baseline

While we'd all like to think that our mind doesn't wander too often, we are often blind to our own habits – especially our negative ones. After all, they're habits, which means that they're happening unconsciously, outside of our awareness.

In order to become aware of your wandering mind, follow these simple steps:

1. Pick a 5 hour period of time where you are doing normal, routine tasks.

2. Copy the chart on the following page into your stroke recovery journal, adding up to 20 rows.

3. Set a timer to go off every 15 minutes.

4. Write down what you happen to be thinking about each time the timer goes off.

5. Try not to pay more attention than normal to where your thoughts are going.

Interval	What I'm Thinking About
1	
2	
3	
4	
5	
6	
7	
8	
9	
10	

While this exercise is rather tedious, it's incredibly useful for discovering more about yourself and your subconscious tendencies. Don't you want to know what your mind is doing when you aren't paying attention to it?

You may be surprised by how many unrelated thoughts are going through your head.

Essential Habit: Write in a Gratitude Journal Daily to Increase Your Resting Happiness

Your 'resting happiness' is the level of happiness that you feel when you're on autopilot. Why should we care about autopilot when we just discussed the importance of turning autopilot off?

Because being 100% present all the time is almost impossible without a lifetime of meditation practice under your belt (like the Buddhist monks). So instead of attempting to do the extreme, you can program your default mode to naturally wander to a positive place, which will uplift your overall sense of happiness.

A great way to do this is through a daily habit of gratitude journaling. You can write in your gratitude journal any way you like. You can write down every single thing you're grateful for until you can't write any more. Or, you can write down as much as you can for just 3 minutes a day. Or, when you're scarce on time, you can just write down 5 things a day, and work your way up from there. It doesn't matter how you do it, as long as you spend some time every day writing about things that you're grateful for.

Some people love the idea of a gratitude journal, while others are suspicious that it will feel repetitive – but that's exactly the point! By repeatedly seeking out the good things in your life, you will strengthen the neural circuits in your brain that are responsible for seeking out the good. Then, as you continue the habit, you will find yourself naturally finding more things to be grateful for even when you're not trying.

That's what happens when you put serious effort into programming a grateful mind. Your brain becomes good at it and will gradually start running this 'gratitude software' even when you're on autopilot. This is a great way to become a naturally happy person.

Chapter 10
Healing Mindfully

"Surrender to what is.

Let go of what was.

Have faith in what will be."

–Sonia Ricotti

In this chapter, we're going to take mindfulness to the next level. But instead of using it to boost our happiness, we're going to use it to boost our self-acceptance through practical tactics like meditation, presence, and breath-movement connection. I will also share a story about a yoga teacher who survived a stroke and demonstrated just how powerful mindfulness can be during recovery.

As you read, try to keep an open mind. Airy-fairy tactics like mindfulness are often shrugged off because they don't seem practical enough to generate results. But I promise that the contents of this chapter have the ability to change the *entire game* during stroke recovery.

Because when you can slow down and live in the present moment, it becomes much easier to make peace with everything that's happening here and now. Mindfulness will help you develop a relationship with the most important person in your world: yourself.

But first, what is mindfulness?

Mindfulness 101

Mindfulness is the art of presence and awareness.

Presence is a state of non-judgement where you're fully absorbed with what's happening in the here and now, not the past or future. Presence involves observing your life with full acceptance of both your inner and outer experiences.

This is important because when we aren't fully present with ourselves, we're not fully engaged with what we're doing. We're away, somewhere else with our thoughts, fluttering around in the past or future. We're not here – and here is the only place where healing happens.

Mindfulness is also the art of *responding* to your environment instead of *reacting* to it.

When we react to our environment, our emotions take a leading role – sometimes irrationally. A reaction puts our first knee-jerk impulse into the world without considering its consequences. And when the leading emotions are negative, we can easily lose control and behave inappropriately.

Responding, however, is less guided by emotion and more focused on reason. While reactions are quick and careless, a response takes more time and thought. And when we take the time to respond, it allows us to consider the consequences of our actions. This allows us to act in accordance with our highest values, which is what we always want. Mindfulness puts you in charge of your reactions, making you less prone to over-reacting and more prone to exercising self-compassion. This is caused by the changes to the brain that mindfulness triggers – specifically from meditation.

Your Brain on Meditation

Your brain takes the shape of whatever patterns you repeatedly practice. By now, you're an expert on this concept. Therefore, when you repeatedly practice accepting the present moment, your brain gets better at acceptance. And the best part is that modern science can show us exactly what that looks like.

During a study on the effects of meditation, a small group of individuals participated in an 8-week mindfulness-based stress reduction course.[6] Neuroscientists took MRI brain scans before and after the study, and the results were shocking.

The study revealed that the mindful meditators increased gray matter concentrations within the left hippocampus, posterior cingulate cortex, temporo-parietal junction, and the cerebellum. To put this in practical terms, meditation helped grow the parts of their brain responsible for learning, memory, emotion regulation, and sense of self!

As Rebecca Gladding, author of *You Are Not Your Brain*, explains, daily meditation can significantly change your brain and help you take things less personally. It can improve the way you interact with others, enhance your compassion, boost your self-acceptance, *and* promote calm centeredness.

Furthermore, adding meditation to your *therapy regimen* has been proven to be more effective than therapy alone. In a study that compared a group of therapy participants who meditated with a group who didn't, those who meditated alongside their therapy improved in the areas of disability, balance, depression, and fatigue.[7]

And if that wasn't enough, sustained meditative practice also helps decrease the size of the amygdala, which, as you know, is the fear center of the brain.

Can you believe that all these benefits come from one simple practice? With more self-compassion and less fear, I hope you can already see the potential that mindfulness has for your recovery.

So the real question is, why aren't we doing more of it?

Don't Let Difficulty Stop You

Meditation is simple. You sit, stand, or lie down and focus your attention into your senses and into your breath, perhaps counting your breaths if you like. You try to avoid thinking – and if you do happen to think, you try to avoid judging it.

You sit there for maybe 2 minutes tops at first, and then grow your practice into 10, maybe 15, minutes of sitting and doing nothing. Sounds absolutely tantalizing, right?

Right?

Exactly.

Meditation may be simple, but it's also hard! It forces you to sit with yourself and get intimate with what's going on underneath. Often, this causes all the repressed emotions from the day (or perhaps *years*) to come bubbling up – and it's *really* uncomfortable.

Because of that, meditation is the easiest thing to put off or avoid altogether. After all, why would we willingly choose to make ourselves uncomfortable?

And that's the key to making your meditation habit stick: choosing discomfort.

We always have two choices in life: stay in comfort or move into growth. By choosing to meditate, you're choosing to grow. You're also choosing to be uncomfortable, antsy, bored, etc., and while we probably don't want to feel that way, those emotions will help you develop yourself. You will outgrow old traits and develop better ones because meditation changes your brain in a myriad of positive ways.

Starting a meditation habit means being willing to be uncomfortable for however long you choose – and that's not an easy choice to make. But when you truly understand how good meditation is – and, better yet, you start to see small changes in your life as a result of your practice – it will help motivate you to keep it up.

If it helps, try to think of meditation as exercise. We know that exercise is good for us, but that doesn't make it easy to do. Exercise is sweaty, exhausting, and makes our muscles burn. But we do it anyway because we know it's good for us. And if we see results, we can become addicted to it – in a good way! But we can only form that addiction if we're 1) willing to be uncomfortable and 2) diligent enough to stick with the habit for the long-run.

So if you sit down to meditate and grow uncomfortable because your mind runs amok, that's normal. Everyone starts off that way. Stick with the habit, stay with yourself, and watch how it helps you grow.

Breath-Movement Connection

After meditation, the next best mindfulness practice is *breath-movement connection*. This is actually a quite simple concept that comes from yoga. If you've ever done yoga, you probably noticed that your instructor frequently reminded you to breathe in while moving one way and to breath out while moving another way. Breathe in and reach up, breathe out and reach down. Breathe in, breathe out. Move one way, then the next.

By moving one way as you inhale and another way as you exhale, you create a rhythm and connection between your breath and your movements. As you practice this for yourself, you may notice that your mind has a hard time wandering because it requires deep focus. And this mind-body focus will pull you into the present moment, which is why it's a great practice to develop mindfulness.

Creating a breath-movement connection can be especially difficult during stroke recovery because some survivors subconsciously hold their breath while they're exercising. In fact, many survivors aren't even aware that they're holding their breath because they're completely focused on moving. Try to avoid that mistake by paying close attention to your breath the next time you exercise. Some therapists say that it can take a survivor 3-4 months to develop breath-movement connection, so be patient with yourself.

I once heard a survivor say to her therapist, "Either I breathe or I move this block, but you can't have both!" Which, of course, made us all laugh. So I know that the breath-movement connection will be a difficult skill to develop, and that's okay. As long as the intention is there, it will come with time and practice.

A Yogi's Recovery

At this point, I would like to share a story about a 51-year-old yoga teacher, Isabelle, who suffered a stroke that left her with right side hemiparesis (severe weakness or partial loss of movement of both her right arm and leg). She had to relearn how to do everything from walking to getting dressed in the morning to brushing her teeth.

Although her initial deficits were significant, Isabelle witnessed how the principles of yoga rapidly moved her recovery along. Remarkably, Isabelle's recovery took just over 3 months!

Isabelle credits the success of her recovery to the healing powers of mindfulness. She also used some of the other concepts we've covered, like banishing limiting beliefs and using visualization techniques. Here are the 5 cornerstones of Isabelle's remarkable recovery:

1. Presence

Yoga is about living in the present moment, and Isabelle was very familiar with this concept. She recognized how important it was for her to focus 100% of her attention on what's happening *now*.

There were times where she wanted to feel angry, but she gave herself *no room* to feel pissed off. All her attention was focused on what she was doing, and this gave her brain the space it needed to heal.

2. Meditation

Yoga and meditation go hand-in-hand. Since Isabelle was a yoga instructor, she had been practicing both for years, and it taught her how to quiet the negative thoughts that cropped up after her stroke. This is a critical point.

Just because she was a yogi that practiced mindfulness didn't mean she never had negative thoughts. However, she was able to recognize them for what they were – *just thoughts*. And she was mindful about replacing them with better ones; thoughts that focused on her accomplishments instead of her anxiety. By displacing her fear, she was able to maintain greater peace of mind throughout her recovery.

3. Breath-Movement Connection

Since breath-movement connection is always emphasized in yoga, Isabelle immediately recognized how important the practice would be during her recovery – but it did *not* come easy.

At first she would lie in bed and practice coordinating her breath with lifting her leg, but she couldn't manage it until after a week of practice. Her therapist, however, said that it was quite the accomplishment, likely due to her previous experience with yoga and breath-movement connection.

4. Limiting Beliefs

Isabelle's neurologist always encouraged Isabelle to try all the things she wanted to do. Although Isabelle's family wanted to shelter her and prevent her from trying things beyond her capabilities, Isabelle's neurologist told her to try anyway and simply stop if she got tired.

Her neurologist understood that if you say you can't do it, then you won't! And if you try, then you will slowly get better.

5. Mind-Body Visualization

Since Isabelle was anxious to get back to yoga, she would spend each night visualizing herself performing one yoga pose, thinking through it from head to toe. Then, the next morning, she would practice the yoga posture and see a tiny bit of progress, which was the small encouragement she needed to keep going.

Isabelle's story is a great reminder that mindfulness and positive psychology both impact your recovery in a big way. If Isabelle had let her negative thoughts consume her or ignored her meditation habit, then she wouldn't have had the successful recovery she achieved.

The mind-body connection is an invaluable tool on your road to recovery. By learning to tune into yourself, you'll have the ability to give your recovery 100% of your attention. And from there, anything is possible.

Exercise: Releasing Mind-Body Resistance

One of the biggest barriers to mindfulness is resistance. Our resistance often starts in our mind in the form of negative thoughts and beliefs, but eventually it can spread into the body. And if we carry resistance within our bodies for long periods of time, it can have a negative impact on our health.

In order to release physical resistance, we first need to become aware of it. How much resistance are you holding on to right now? Let's find out.

As you read this, take a deep breath in and, as you exhale, allow your entire body to relax from head to toe. Allow your scalp to relax. Allow your face to relax. Let your shoulders relax down your back. Continue to take deep, mindful breaths. Then allow your back and stomach to release any tension. Allow your legs to relax. And finally, allow your feet to relax. Take another deep breath in, and let it all go.

Was there a big change in your body from before you read that paragraph until now? If so, then you know what you need to work on: relaxing your mind so that your body can relax too.

Exercise: Self-Acceptance Affirmations

Affirmations are effective for two reasons. First, they use neuroplasticity to rewire your mind to believe whatever you're affirming. Second, affirmations are thoughts. And, going back to the Framework, you know that all thoughts lead to feelings. By generating affirming thoughts, you can create the feeling of self-acceptance, which will inevitably lead to self-caring behaviors and results.

However, affirmations only work if they're believable. If you start with a belief that's too outlandish, then you will be running two mental loops at once: one that is creating the affirmation, and another that is defeating it by labeling the affirmation as stupid and unrealistic. Try not to do that. Have faith that affirmations are a great way to rewire your mind and generate more self-acceptance.

Now that you understand why affirmations are effective, let's put them into practice. For this exercise, try reciting each of these affirmations aloud at least 10 times. Try to work your way up to fifty repetitions each, but keep a minimum of ten as your baseline.

I release all resistance to the present moment.

I release all emotions that do not serve me.

I release all thoughts that do not serve me.

151

I am willing to accept the present moment.

I accept myself unconditionally, exactly as I am right now.

I am at peace with myself.

I welcome change into my life with enthusiasm.

I surrender to this present moment.

Some of these affirmations, like "I accept myself unconditionally," may be very hard to say right now, and that's okay. We *all* have difficulty saying the things that we don't quite believe yet.

If you feel resistance, use it as an indicator of which affirmations you need to prioritize. Don't give up on an affirmation just because it doesn't feel good. In fact, that's probably the one you need the most!

And in time, the good feelings will come.

Essential Habit: Meditate Daily to Increase Self-Acceptance

Meditation will change your brain in positive ways and improve your recovery. So practicing daily is a must.

There are countless meditation techniques available, and I encourage you to do a little research and find one that resonates with you. For starters, you can try the 4-7-8 technique.

To perform this meditation, inhale for a count of 4 breaths, hold your breath at the top for a count of 7, and then exhale for a count of 8. Repeat this four times, and work your way up from there. If this feels uncomfortable or overwhelming, you can always try a different technique.

Now, how can we make meditation a habit?

A great trick is to link your meditation practice with a daily cue – something that you do every day. For example, if you're a coffee drinker, then turn your morning coffee into a cue to meditate. It will serve as a necessary reminder for a lasting habit.

Most importantly, no matter how difficult or frustrating meditation may feel – don't give up! It will get easier with consistent practice. It doesn't matter if you sit there thinking about a bunch of different things for two minutes. The process of *staying with yourself* – whether your mind is silent or running amok – is what matters.

And as long as you're there and you're *committed*, your brain is changing for the better.

Chapter 11
Returning to Love

"You yourself, as much as anybody
in the entire universe, deserve your
love and affection."

–The Buddha

In the very beginning of this book, I said: "If you love your recovery, your recovery will love you back. But you can only get there by loving yourself *first*." And that's what this final chapter is all about.

Now, *why on earth* would I put the first part last? Because self-love is unfortunately the hardest part. It requires self-understanding, self-acceptance, patience, and a positive mindset. In other words, it takes everything that we've covered to get there.

So, here we are. Right back where we started. Only, this time we're equipped with the tools we need to make the whole process easier.

This chapter will help you find self-love by addressing the top three barriers that stand in its way: shame, self-criticism, and body resentment. And once these barriers are revealed, you can finally work towards the self-love you deserve.

Loving Yourself First

Before we dive into the specifics, let me explain what I mean by "loving yourself first."

Unfortunately, we often delay loving ourselves until we achieve some desired level of adequacy. We wait until we get that job back, we lose those 10 pounds, or we achieve that full recovery. But in the meantime, we're missing out on the momentum and energy that self-love brings, which can help us move towards those goals.

Everything in life works better when you put your thoughts and feelings *before* your actions. The Framework showed us that.

So what would happen if you started loving yourself now instead of waiting until you achieved the results you want? Your results would come easier – that's for sure. Because instead of waiting to feel better in order to love yourself, you will love yourself into feeling better.

And you don't have to wait for *anything* in order to love yourself. You don't have to wait until your deficits are gone.

You don't have to wait until you get your old life back. You don't have to wait until you get one inch further.

You can begin loving yourself *today*.

The following steps are a great place to start.

Step 1: Identifying Shame

"In order to love who you are, you cannot hate the experiences that shaped you."

–Andrea Dykstra

The greatest barrier to self-love is shame, which is a self-destructive emotion that makes us feel like we are lacking, incompetent, and unlovable.

Whenever we feel like we aren't enough, that's shame showing its ugly head. Whenever we're afraid to be vulnerable, that's shame standing in our way. Whenever we veer away from challenge because we're afraid of what other people will think, that's shame preventing us from achieving our full potential.

In order to find self-love, we can't equate struggle, failure, or disability with being unworthy of love. In fact, those are the very things that make us worthy of love! To have the courage to show up each day and make ourselves vulnerable even when we're struggling and recovering from life-changing events – that's the *essence* of love.

Unfortunately, shame separates us from that. And the worst part is that we often keep it hidden. No one enjoys talking about their shame (at first). But the less we talk about it, the more power it has. Being afraid to speak our truth is shame's primary source of fuel.

Luckily, this means that if we can generate enough awareness about shame to identify it and talk about it, we've basically stripped it of all its power. But if we can dethrone shame this easily, then why aren't we all doing it?

Unhealthy Ways We Cope with Shame

When we're shameful, the last thing we want to do is talk about it. Instead, it's much easier to hide and wait for it to be over. But the easy route is also more painful. Without giving a voice to our shame, it remains invisible.

We remain invisible.

As a consequence, we avoid challenging ourselves because we don't want to risk exposure. Shame causes us to hide because we're afraid of being 'found out.' We believe, often at a subconscious level, that others will exploit our weaknesses if we make ourselves vulnerable. So we hide. Sometimes we hide behind the illusion of being okay, and sometimes we literally just tuck ourselves away.

However, isolation isn't the only way that shame manifests. It's just the most popular. There are two others ways that shame manifests.

First, some people cope with shame by becoming chronic people pleasers. They bend over backwards to get approval from others because it gives them validation that they cannot give themselves.

Second, some cope with shame by using coercion and force to gain power over others. This often manifests in aggressive behavior that fights shame with shame, which only worsens it.

But enough talk about the problem. Let's talk about the solution.

Shame Ends with a Story

"When you own the story,
you get to write the ending."

–Brene Brown

The first step to dissolving shame is simply recognizing it. This can be difficult if you've been living with shame for long periods of time. However, understanding the ways that shame manifests can help you identify any shameful patterns in your own behavior.

Then, once you've identified your pain, talk about it. *Tell your story.* The only thing that fuels our shame is the fact that we keep it hidden. When we wrap words and a story around our shame, it dissolves. Without secrecy, shame cannot exist.

So, own it. Own your story and speak your whole truth. If this sounds terrifying, then be sure to share your story with someone who will respond with *empathy* and understanding, like close friends or other stroke survivors. Share your story and secrets with those who will comfort you and say, "I understand you. I've been in a similar place. You are not alone."

One great way to do this is by starting your own blog. I've seen many stroke survivor start their own recovery blogs to document their journey. Not only does this provide a nice record of your timeline, accomplishments, and lessons, but it's also the perfect place to share your story.

Often, telling your story to a group of strangers is much less terrifying than telling those closest to you. So if the idea of telling your story to a blank online audience sounds interesting, then do it! Chances are, other stroke survivors will find it and chime in with a chorus of, "I understand you. I am in a similar place. You are not alone."

And if you don't think this would give you the feedback you need, then try writing your story anyway, but keep it private. Then share it with those closest to you. Sometimes it's much easier to say, "Hey, here's my story. Read it and understand me," than actually rehashing the whole thing in person.

The important thing is to find an outlet that suits your needs, and then *speak your truth*. All that matters is telling your story to someone who will listen with empathy. When we speak our truth and feel heard while we do it, that's when we find freedom from shame.

Step 2: Ending Self-Criticism

The second biggest barrier to self-love is self-criticism, which is the negative way we talk to ourselves. Whenever we beat ourselves up over something, we give shame a little more fuel, and we also move a little farther away from ourselves.

We cannot love ourselves and bring ourselves down at the same time. Self-love is compassionate, kind, and empowering. Self-criticism is demoralizing, discouraging, and defeating.

Sometimes we aren't even aware of how hard we are on ourselves, either. A good way to determine if self-criticism is a problem for you is by watching how you criticize others. Are you hard on the people around you, like your children or coworkers? Do you judge other people and make comments on what they're doing?

If so, it's crucial to understand that we are only as hard on others as we are on ourselves. We also tend to judge other people in the same areas that we are vulnerable to shame ourselves. For example, if you find yourself judging other peoples' bodies, then it's an indication that you may be particularly hard on yourself about your own body.

This means that watching our own judgmental thoughts about others can help us identify the areas where we judge *ourselves*. And once we find these wounds, we need to heal them with loving self-talk.

That's the first cure to self-criticism: talking compassionately to the parts of yourself that you criticize the most. Try to talk in the same way that you would talk to someone you love and are trying to comfort in the midst of a meltdown.

For example, if you're feeling particularly embarrassed about something, you can tell yourself, "It's okay. I'm okay. I'm human and we all make mistakes. And whether or not I make the same mistake again, I will always have my back." Compassionate self-talk like this is the foundation of self-love.

The second cure to self-criticism is identifying which *values* are triggering that criticism. Often, we're hard on ourselves because we're attempting to live up to a self-image we have in our head. And when that image is causing pain, it's best to just drop it.

For example, if you value having an attractive body but you don't feel like you have one, then that could be the cause of your self-criticism. You aren't living up to your values, and it triggers shame.

Therefore, in this example, it's best to just drop the value of having an attractive body and replace that value with something that promotes *inner strength*. For instance, values like courage, compassion, and persistence are excellent values to uphold.

And when you uphold values that strengthen you from *within*, you can see someone with a nice body and find the capacity to say, "I used to desire a body like that, but appearance is not a value that drives me anymore. I value compassion and I'm going to be compassionate towards the body I have." Not only does this put self-criticism to bed, but it also puts shame to rest, too.

Exercise: List 50 Things You Love About Yourself

Another great way to put self-criticism to rest is to train yourself to recognize how loveable you already are. You are overflowing with things to love. It's just hard to see sometimes because our dang negativity bias keeps us fixated on the wrong things. It's a sad truth, but we're about to work on it.

For this exercise, write down 50 things you love about yourself. Don't pay attention to how fast or slow you complete the exercise. It takes almost everyone an uncomfortably long amount of time to complete the first time around.

So ignore the clock and just focus on how you feel about what you're writing. Are you surprised by how much there is to love about yourself? Are you unable to find 50 things to love? If so, try doing this exercise every day for one month.

It may feel excessive or narcissistic, but the repetition is necessary – and it's *not* narcissistic. Narcissism is the belief that you are better than others. Self-love is the belief that *you are enough*. And there is nothing wrong with performing a daily exercise to reinforce that essential belief.

Step 3: Forgiving Your Body

The third greatest barrier to self-love is resentment. When we feel like we've been wronged by others, resentment can build. And when we feel like we've been wronged by our *own body*, self-resentment can build – and that's the worst kind of all.

When we live in a body that we haven't forgiven, we abandon ourselves. We sever the relationship that we have with our body – the only home we will ever truly have – and allow resentment, frustration, and anger to fester inside the very thing that is causing our pain.

Our bodies don't respond well to self-loathing. Our bodies need compassion and understanding. Otherwise, rehabilitation will move like sludge. Each day will be full of harsh, unsuccessful commands to a body that simply won't listen. But when we soften our voice and learn to speak to our bodies with compassion instead – it listens. And we heal much faster that way.

There's plenty of science supporting this, too. For example, studies show that the state of unforgiveness can cause health risks and depression, while forgiveness reverses these negative effects *and* provides other positive benefits, such as increased empathy, compassion, and hope.[8] In other words, all the things that promote self-love!

As you can see, nothing moves with the feelings of resentment. Everything moves with love and forgiveness. Both the scientists and the sages are clear on this one: *We need forgiveness in order to heal.*

We need to forgive our bodies so that we can recover properly. We need to rebuild a beautiful relationship with ourselves so that we can embrace our bodies exactly as they are. Body forgiveness is *essential* for self-love.

Luckily, it's not a complicated process. All you need to do is recognize any body resentment festering inside, and then make the decision to *let it go*. Let the resentment fade away like the last cloud on a hot summer day.

To help expedite the process, you can also try repeating this affirmation aloud:

"I forgive my body."

Saying these words out loud will help them seep into your belief system. It may feel foreign at first, but stay with the process. Your body is always listening to you, and when you speak compassionately to it, it will respond.

Some people experience a slight lightness in their body after repeating this affirmation, as if the release of resentment acts as the release of a physical burden. For others, it can take days/weeks/*months* to finally release their body resentment.

Don't judge yourself for wherever you are in this process. All that matters is that you're working on healing your relationship with your body. Setting that intention and repeating the affirmation is already a huge step in the right direction.

Exercise: Write a Compassionate Letter to Your Body

To continue releasing body resentment, a great exercise is to write a compassionate letter to your body. And if you don't have the ability to write yet, then you can do this same exercise with a voice recorder. It may feel silly, but it's *surprisingly* therapeutic.

Start the letter by stating that you forgive your body for causing your stroke; that you forgive it for not cooperating when you want it to; and you're thankful for all the hard work it's doing. Then let the rest of the letter flow freely. Say what you need to say and let it all hang out.

As you write, be sure to use the same words that you would use with a close friend. Be gentle, caring, and compassionate. Let your body know that you feel betrayed and that you're also going to work with it instead of against it from here on out.

Practicing Self-Love

Now that you are aware of the three barriers to self-love, you can begin your practice. And like all things, it really is a practice. One that you must honor *daily*. Practicing self-love means practicing self-care, self-acceptance, and self-compassion at all times. As you know, three great places to start are: owning your story, speaking kindly to yourself, and forgiving your body.

Having the courage to choose truth, compassion, and forgiveness is how we choose love. And you cannot make these choices once and expect them to stick forever. They must be honored every single day.

As you begin to tell your story, you will learn to stand behind yourself no matter what. As you live according to your highest truth, you will learn to own every inch of who you are. As you forgive your body, you will learn to own your space.

Slowly but surely, through these self-loving practices, you will develop strength and courage and bravery. You will fuel your ability to recover from stroke and grow closer to yourself during the process. Instead of questioning your worth, you will learn to stand up in your worthiness – and in love.

And when you love yourself, true healing and happiness is possible.

Essential Habit: Applying This Book

Congrats! You've made it to the end! But we're far from being done.

Reading and understanding this book is one thing, but *doing* this book is another. In order to start creating change in your life, it's important to deliberately apply the concepts.

For your last essential habit, make a point of spending at least 5 minutes a day applying the concepts in this book. This will help you avoid the easy trap of learning information and filing it away without doing anything. The only way to grow is to learn *and* apply. The second step is even more critical than the first.

To learn the skills of confidence and self-love and recovery, you need to actively apply your knowledge again and again and again. Repetitive practice is how you will create positive change.

So before you put this book away, dive back in and try doing the exercises that you were excited about – they're probably the ones you need the most. If one chapter resonated with you more than the rest, start there! Start by tackling shame first, or start by tackling fear first. Or start with those new emotions.

Be creative with the little nuggets of knowledge that you took away from this book. This is your fresh start, and you get to make whatever you want out of it.

So, it's your turn now. Go read and apply, heal and be happy, and watch how you fall in love.

With yourself and your recovery.

References

1. Biernaskie, J., Chernenko, G. & Corbett, D. Efficacy of rehabilitative experience declines with time after focal ischemic brain injury. *J. Neurosci.* **24,** 1245–1254 (2004).

2. Nilsen, D. M., Gillen, G. & Gordon, A. M. Use of mental practice to improve upper-limb recovery after stroke: a systematic review. *Am. J. Occup. Ther.* **64,** 695–708 (2010).

3. Page, S. J. Mental practice: A promising practice technique in stroke rehabilitation. *J. Sport Exerc. Psychol.* **24,** 13–14 (2002).

4. Braun, S. M., Beurskens, A. J., Borm, P. J., Schack, T. & Wade, D. T. The Effects of Mental Practice in Stroke Rehabilitation: A Systematic Review. *Arch. Phys. Med. Rehabil.* **87,** 842 852 (2006).

5. Killingsworth, M. A. & Gilbert, D. T. A Wandering Mind Is an Unhappy Mind. *Science.* **330,** 932–932 (2010).

6. Gotink, R. A., Meijboom, R., Vernooij, M. W., Smits, M. & Hunink, M. G. M. 8-week Mindfulness Based Stress Reduction induces brain changes similar to traditional long-term meditation practice: A systematic review. *Brain Cogn.* **108,** 32–41 (2016).

7. John, S., Khanna, G. L. & Kotwal, P. Effect of music therapy and meditation along with conventional physiotherapy management in sub-acute stroke patients. *Br. J. Sports Med.* **44,** i14 (2010).

8. Toussaint, L. L., Shields, G. S. & Slavich, G. M. Forgiveness, Stress, and Health: a 5-Week Dynamic Parallel Process Study. *Ann. Behav. Med.* **50,** 727–735 (2016).